AF540849

Poor and Development

POOR AND DEVELOPMENT

By
Dr. M. Lakshmi Narasaiah
M.A., Ph.D.
Professor & Head
Department of Economics
Sri Krishnadevaraya University Post-graduate Centre
Kurnool–518 002
Andhra Pradesh (India)

DISCOVERY PUBLISHING HOUSE
NEW DELHI

First Published–2004

ISBN: 81-7141-761-2

Published by:

DISCOVERY PUBLISHING HOUSE

4831/24, Prahlad Street, Ansari Road, Darya Ganj
New Delhi–110 002 (India)
Phone: 23279245, • Fax: 91-11-23253475
e-mail: dphtemp@indiatimes.com

Printed at:

Tarun Offset Printers, Delhi-53

Preface

Will the international target of reducing poverty by half over the next 15 years be met? Not unless growth efforts are accompanied by significant improvements in income distribution. Poverty reduction is a twin function of the rate of growth and of changes in income distribution. The research shows better distribution has as much impact on reducing poverty as had increased growth. And given predicted rates of economic growth, it emerges as the factor that will make the main difference between success and failure for new 'pro-poor' growth strategies.

Over the past decade, the amount of poverty reduction resulting from a given rate of economic growth has varied in close step with income distribution. On average, a growth rate of 10 per cent reduced the poverty headcount (the percentage of people living on less than $ 1 a day) by 9 per cent in countries where income was fairly equally distributed. However in countries where income was unequally distributed, a growth rate of 10 per cent reduced the poverty headcount by only 3 per cent.

The World Bank estimates that developing countries will grow at 4 per cent per capital per annum until 2015. So the good news is that the income-poverty target is attainable provided that significant improvements take place in income distribution. These can be achieved ex-ante, by designing growth strategies that increase disproportionately the incomes of the poorest, or ex-post, by redistributing income through taxation. Many questions arise. What is the recipe for income-redistributing growth? Is there a trade-off between growth and distribution? An ex-post strategies of reduction feasible? These questions are far from new. Indeed, to a large degree, they are the very questions on which the development studies profession is founded. Nevertheless, they have been neglected in recent years. Does current research offer new perspectives? Articles in this issue of insights offer six main conclusions. They are that:

- We need a way to measure 'pro-poor growth'. The concept originates from the 1990 World Development Report of the World Bank and is taken to mean a labour intensive growth path that encompasses the economic activities of the poor. However, such a growth path could be accompanied by increasing, declining or static income inequality. McCulloch and Baulch propose that the 'poverty bias of growth' or PBG (whether pro-poor or not) be defined by comparing actual change in income distribution with the change that would have resulted had all incomes grown at one rate with no change to income inequality. This difference is compared in their report (opposite) for two states in India. From this comparison it emerges that growth in Bihar State was accompanied by worsening income distribution and has been biased against the poor, whereas in Andhra Pradesh the reverse was true.

- Growth might be expected to be pro-poor if it takes place in areas and sectors where the poor live and work. For the poorest countries this means mostly in rural areas and to a large extent in agriculture. In Asia, Green Revolution technologies were adopted by poor farmers because they were scale-neutral and low-risk. Poor non-farmers also benefited from the extra employment and lower food prices that resulted. In Sub-Saharan Africa, the Green Revolution has been slower in coming, but research at Reading by Mosley suggests an African Green Revolution will help. In Uganda, for example, the spread to new technologies in maize and cassava has contributed to sharp falls in poverty, notable in the country's North, where mosaic-resistant cassava has made a conspicuous difference to farmer's yields and incomes in an otherwise poor and undeveloped region.

- Even so, as many will remember well from debates

about the Green Revolution in Asia, not everybody benefits from growth. In Ethlopia, researchers from the Universities of Oxford and Addis Ababa found that rural poverty has fallen sharply since the change of government in 1992, driven by market liberalisation and better weather (see Dercon, backfold). Yet those who have gained have been those with assets, including land, oxen for ploughing, education and access to public goods such as roads. Those without assets are left behind. Rural inequality has actually risen, implying Ethiopia could reduce poverty faster if policies countered inequality yet maintained current growth rates.

- People without assets might be expected to compensate by migrating or moving out of agriculture. Sometimes this happens, but seeking off-farm opportunities may be easier for the haves than the have-nots. In rural Zimbabwe, for example, Piesse and Thirtie have shown that (in more remote areas at least) those with higher farm incomes are better placed to exploit off-farm opportunities, including the option of working in town.

- In any case, migration to town may not offer much to the unskilled—again, a-problem facing those without assets. The evidence here comes from China, in research carried out by the Institute of Economics and Statistics. Wage employment has increased in urban China, but wage inequality has increased sharply, with falling real wages for the unskilled.

- The efficiency (hence the growth) and equity trade-off is far from clear cut. Analysis by Knight of the reasons behind rising wage income inequality in China has revealed that some of these changes reflect greater labour market efficiency. In other words, more productive, experienced and skilled workers have become better paid. Other chages hint at new inefficiencies creeping into China's labour market, such as growing labour market, such as growing discrimination: females and minority groups find they are disadvantaged in the labour market, whereas members of the Communist Party are more likely to get jobs. Other signs are sharper segmentation, with state employees paid more than private sector counterparts and growing differences in wage rates between the provinces, not offset by labour mobility.

The cross-section of findings offered in these pages do not amount to a systematic review of the 'inequality question' in developing countries. Far from it: here is fertile ground for further research. Even so, we are confident that it is time to promote inequality to the fore of the research and policy agenda.

Dr. M. Lakshmi Narasaiah

Contents

Chapter—1

Resistance to Change

Why Poverty Reduction Programmes Did Not Work

Poverty reduction as an overall objective of the global development industry is not new. The only problem is that so far it has not really worked. Despite several decades of economic growth and huge development aid disbursements, the number of countries the United Nations calls "least developed" (those with a per capita income of less than US$ 900 a year) has in fact nearly doubled since 1971, from 25 to 49. In the last decade (1990-2000) and despite all development efforts—not even one country was able to graduate from this group to a higher income level, maybe with the exception of Botswana.

Meanwhile, poverty reduction has generated its own history. This programme has covered a wide range of approaches starting from the World Bank's small-farmers-strategies in the 1970's via the costly structural adjustment policies of the 1980's to the recent poverty reduction strategies of the 1990's. Once more, the next development decade (2000-2010) has written "Attacking Poverty" on its banner. It seems that something must have gone wrong along the way. What (bitter?) lessons have been learnt from previous experience? Have they been factored into the new set of policies? Were there possibly some fundamental flaws which were overlooked, and can better results be expected during the next period? Or do the many failures and disappointments demonstrate that there is some systemic "resistance to change" by those in power in the least developed countries and perhaps also by the poor themselves?

1. What can the rural poor really expect from poverty reduction programmes?

In India, for example, 70 per cent of the people still earn their livelihood in the agricultural sector; most of the poor among them live in a kind of rural subsistence economy. People who live in a subsistence economy are naturally conservative. They are busy securing their survival and are very reluctant to take risks. Their living standard is measured in amounts of rice harvested; their wealth is measured in numbers of livestock. Within this simple framework, poor peasants behave very rationally. For example, a shift from food crops to cash crops, such as from rice to coffee or tapioca, would immediately endanger their subsistence in case of failure. Furthermore, the poor do not have the knowledge and skills to change their crops quickly in response to market demands. Moving from a subsistence economy to a commodity economy is therefore a big step for small farmers.

However, poor people are always happy to receive handouts from the government like fertilizer, seeds, medicine or blankets. Roads, bridges and schools are also very welcome. Who would refuse a gift? From their point of view, it is the responsibility of the government to distribute goods and services in form of aid programmes as a way to share some of the prosperity of the city people with them. Nevertheless, as they see no direct and immediate benefit for themselves, they tend to take a rather passive attitude to change. Development workers have often complained about this common apathy and about the lack of will among the poor themselves to improve their situation. In the final analysis, rural development is more a problem of providing the right economic incentives for change than of overcoming traditional thinking and a conservative attitude.

2. What kind of incentives are necessary to achieve increased production in the countryside?

In most poor countries the key to rural development is the problem of land ownership rights and of legal security. As long as people do not own the land that they cultivate, they are not interested in making any investments, be they in the form of labour or capital. Once a farmer has an ownership title and considers the land as his own, he will refrain from over-using the soil but shift crops and plant new trees. Moreover, he can then use his land as collateral for credits or even sell it and buy land somewhere else.

In addition to clear and irrevocable ownership rights, the rule of law is another crucial factor for development. People must feel safe from abuse of power by local elites and corrupt government officials. They must be able to enforce their basic rights in an impartial court of law. Furthermore, they must be safe from land expropriation without adequate compensation and from resettlement against their will. In other words, it is primarily their very stake holdership in the rural economy that will motivate them to increase their production. Of course, the other necessary incentives are access to market, a fair price for their products and the availability of goods and services.

3. Poverty reduction programmes, if not accompanied by parallel institutional reforms, run the risk of creating a modern version of the cargo cult.

Cargo cults spread during World War II in the highlands of Papua New Guinea at a time when several US cargo planes loaded with food supplies crashed into the hills. Suddenly, the native people could enjoy an abundant amount of goods, which literally fell down on them like a "gift from heaven". In the hope of attracting some more of these "silvery birds", the local hilltribes constructed primitive models of airplanes, sat around them in a circle, and prayed that more "cargo" would drop on their territory. As this happened in some areas (albeit as a result of the air battle between Japan and the USA), it strengthened the belief in the cargo cult as some magical way to overcome poverty—at least for a short time.

There is a high risk that aid programmes under the banner of poverty reduction will create new "cargo cults" in the 49 least developed countries if they continue to carry out their "business as usual" and do not put strong emphasis on the rule of law and civil rights. Unfortunately, the setting up of reliable legal and social institutions in poor countries (which often seems to be the "software" of the development industry accompanying disbursements) is, in fact, as decades of experience have shown, the hard part of the process. But it is also indispensable for achieving any tangible results.

Why have there been until now only modest results in the areas of land reform, rule of law and the guarantee of basic civil rights? Why have people's participation and people's ownership as a strategy hardly taken root at all in the least developed countries? The answer must be sought in the role of powerful local groups and their vested interests, who obviously benefit form the prevailing status quo and a loose legal environment. A cargo cult promises bounty for all recipients; poverty reduction, however, means changing the rural power structure, too.

Conclusion

To insist on the rule of law, on people's participation in the development process, and on transparency and accountability, is again nothing new. Good political and administrative institutions go hand in hand with economic growth. The potential of economic development is quite limited if it works in a framework of social undevelopment and official indifference. Again the question is, who has so little been achieved in this field during previous decades? Was it the wrong medicine and why were the poor results of the aid programmes so carefully ignored by the international donor community?

Looking at the political systems of the 49 least developed countries, it is abvious that most of these countries are "more democratic in principle than in practice". Many of them are ruled by military or civil authoritarian regimes which are more used to giving orders than to listening to the grievances of the poor. Other governments, such as India, are "genuinely democratic at most levels but have historically found it difficult that political accountability reaches all levels of decision making, particularly for the poor".

To sum up, it seems that resistance to change is equally shared by the cumbersome and often incompetent bureaucracies of the poor countries and the equally cumbersome international donor community, which has so far conveniently kept the call for more rural democracy and people's rights on the backburner.

The major reason for the reluctance of the donor community to pursue the battle for the rule of law and the fight against endemic corruption was to avoid massive political confrontation with the receiver countries.

Would it not have been better to create proper incentives for the performance of poor countries, namely by halting loans to nations that do not manage their economies and their reform commitments effectively and increasing financial and technical support to those that do? The next decade will show how determined both local governments and donors are to tackle these problems for the sake of a better future.

Chapter—2

Private Education

The Poor's Best Chance

Across the developing world, private schools and education companies are not only flourishing, but reaching the poor. India is a case in point. A common assumption about the private sector in education is that it caters only to the elite, and that its promotion only serves to exacerbate inequality. On the contrary recent research points in the opposite direction. If we want to help some of the most disadvantages groups in society, then encouraging deeper private sector involvements is likely to be the best way forward.

Several developments are underway in India, all of which involve the private education sector meeting the needs of the poor in distinct ways. But India is not unique is this respect—similar phenomena are happening all over the developing world.

As a point of departure, how do government schools serve the poor? Usefully, the government sponsored Public Report on Basic Education in India (PROBE) from 1999 paints a very bleak picture of the "malfunctioning" of government schools for the poor. When researchers called unannounced on their random sample of schools, only 53 per cent had any 'teaching activity' going on. In 33 per cent, the head teacher was absent. Alarmingly, the team noted that the deterioration of teaching standards was not to do with disempowered teachers, but instead could be ascribed to "plain negligence". They noted "several cases of irresponsible teachers keeping a school closed... for months at a time," many cases of drunk teachers, and head teachers who asked children to do domestic chores. Significantly, the low level of teaching activity occurred even in those schools with relative good infrastructure, teaching aids and pupil-teacher ratios.

But is there any alternative to these schools? Surely no one else can do better than government given the resources available? As it happens, the PROBE report was serving the poor and conceded—rather reluctantly—such problems were not found in these schools. In the great majority of private schools—again visited unannounced and at random—there "was feverish classroom activity." Most parents would prefer to send their children to private schools if they could afford them. Private schools, they said, were successful because they were more accountable: "the teachers are accountable to the manager (who can fire them), and, through him or her, to the parents (who can withdraw their children)." Such accountability was not present in the government schools, and "this contrast is perceived with crystal clarity by the vast majority of parents".

The Way Forward: Loosen Regulations and Set up Voucher Schemes

To many readers, the existence of these private schools for the poor will come as a surprise. It was to me too, until I had the privilege of conducting field work for the International Finance Corporation (the private finance arm of the World Bank) on a group of such schools operating under the banner of the Federation of Private Schools management based in Hyderabad. The federation has 500 private schools (from kindergarten to grade ten) serving poor communities in slums and villages. I was impressed by both the entrepreneurial spirit within these schools—they were run on commercial principles, not dependent on hand-outs from state or philanthropy—but also by the spirit of dedication within the schools for the poor communities served: not for nothing were the leaders of the schools known as "social workers". But these schools suffer under restrictive and inappropriate regulations. One example will suffice: to be recognized a school must deposit upto Rs. 50,000 (about $1.200) in a stipulated bank account, of which neither the capital nor the interest can be touched. Given that the fees charged in these schools ranged from 25 (60 cents) to Rs. 150 per month (about $3.50) with most of the schools grouped near the lower end of the range, such sums are completely prohibitive.

Fees of around $10 per year are not affordable by everyone, but they are to a large number of poor families. Furthermore, the great majority of the schools offer a significant number of free places—up to 20 per cent—for the poorest students, allocated on the basis of claims of need checked informally in the community.

All of this suggests that if one is interested in serving the needs of the poor in India, then trying to reform the totally inadequate, cumbersome and unaccountable government system is unlikely to be the best way. Instead, reform the regulatory environment to make it suitable for the flourishing of private schools for the poor, help build private financing schemes using overseas and indigenous philanthropy, and encourage public voucher schemes so that parents can use their allowance of funding where they see the schools are performing well, rather than wasting them in unresponsive state schools.

Private education in developing countries isn't just about the poor, of course, and there are many exciting examples of big education businesses. But these too have implications for the ways in which the private sector can reach the least advantaged. One Indian company which embodies much of the excite the National Institute for Information Technology (NIIT). With its competitor, Aptech, it shares just over 70 per cent of the information technology education and training market in India estimated at roughly Rs.1.1 billion ($24 million). NIIT has 40 wholly owned centres in the metropolitan areas, and about 1,000 franchised centres across India. It also has a global reach, with centres in the U.S., Asian Pacific, Europe, Japan, Central Asia and Africa. A key aspect of NIIT's educational philosophy is that there is a need to harness research to improve the efficiency of learning and to raise educational standards.

Because of its success in developing innovative and cost-effective IT education and training, NIIT has attracted the attention of several state governments. First off the mark was Tamil Nadu, which wanted to bring a computer curriculum to all of its high schools. Significantly, although allocating about $22 million over five years to this endeavour, it didn't hand the funds over to government schools, perhaps in light of the PROBE report's lessons. Instead, it developed a model to contract out the service to private companies, which provide the software and hardware, while the government supplies electricity and the class-room. For the first round of the Tamil Nadu process, 43 contracts were awarded for 666 schools, with NIIT allotted 371 schools. Many of the classrooms have become NIIT centre, open to school children and teachers in daytime, then used by the franchise holder in the evenings. The contracting out of curriculum areas such as this represents an important step forward in relationships between the public and private sectors, and provides an interesting model worth watching and emulating.

Most recently, NIIT has focused on reaching largely illiterate and unschooled children through the internet. Within weeks of having set up an "internet kiosk" in a slum area, the institute's researchers found that without any instruction, children could achieve a remarkable level of computer literacy. NIIT is exploring ways to roll out the idea commercially, harnessing the power of the private sector to reach the poorest through modern technology.

These initiatives all find echoes in other developing countries. In each case, the private, not the public sector, is most responsive to the needs of the poor, and is bringing innovation, efficiency and educational quality to the lives of the most disadvantaged. The private sector has the potential to promote greater equity and to influence education policy, provided it is encouraged and viewed as a partner, not a threat to governments, whether in the developing or the developed world.

Chapter—3
Unemployment in the Poor and Rich Worlds

Different Causes, but Converging Policies?

In view of the magnitude of global unemployment, all the customary formulas offered by economists against mass unemployment—the basic socio-economic problem of modern times—appear to be quackery. Neither quantitative, nor any kind of 'qualitative' growth will be able to eliminate the disastrous worldwide lack of jobs. For ecological reasons it is impossible to include 800 million or more unemployed in the production process through corresponding growth. The resulting increase in global Gross Domestic Product would require consumption of natural resources, energy and the environment which, given even the greatest possible productivity in those sectors, could not even be sustained for two or three decades.

In addition, aiming to achieve full employment through growth will be ever more difficult even in the rich economies. For it is most likely that work productivity will continue to rise worldwide. Countries such as China, which are in the initial phase of modernisation, are still producing at a relatively still low productivity rate. But that is precisely why they can achieve notable increases in productivity in a short time by importing technology from highly-developed countries. The advantage of rapid 'catch-up rationalisation', however, is being bought at the cost of rising unemployment and progressive impoverishment.

Employment through Redistribution of Work

The notion that jobs can at some time be created for 800-900 million unemployed who will work 35 or even 40 hours a week at the productivity level of the highly-developed countries of four or five decades ago is absurd. The only realistic possibility of eliminating the world's unemployment problem is by far-reaching redistribution of work and income. The change needed for that demands fundamentally new concepts of prosperity: a reflection on the philosophy of the 'life of happiness'. 'New concepts of prosperity' means that technological progress would no longer by used mainly to deliver rising per capita incomes and excessive consumption. Instead, given a sufficient material standard of living, the quality of life would be improved primarily by shortening working hours. It is about, so to speak, assigning instrumental good sense new goals. Plus reshaping socio-economic conditions in such a way that the politicians with again be compelled to orient themselves on the good of the community and humanistic values instead of filling the pockets of the wealthy. It is sheer ideology, although very persuasive, to cite 'globalisation' and its alleged 'iron laws' in defaming the welfare state, full employment and social justice as out-of-date wishful thinking. A return to the state-guided social competitive system as practised during the first decades after the Second World War is possible just as it was politically feasible to make the transition from the old order of unfettered, ruthless capitalism to the mixed economies of the social market economy types. So it is a matter of restoring the proven structures of a mixed economic system.

However, in contrast to the first post-war decades it is now not sufficient to regenerate nation-state interventionism. Appropriate international regulations are required. Above all, it will depend upon reversing the new laissez-faire developments in international economic relationships which today are subsumed under the buzzword 'globalisation'. That is, to oppose over-liberalisation and its disastrous social and inhuman impacts. It will depend on the broad mobilisation of the losers in the process of globalisation whether the necessary fundamental change of course can still be made in time before a catastrophe. In particular, the new myth must be opposed that declares globalisation as a kind of law of nature and thus suggests resignation and adaptation to an allegedly unavoidable process of destruction of social and human achievements.

Mass Unemployment in the Poor Economies

The employment problems in the rich and the poor hemispheres differ not only in their magnitude, but also in their causes. The wretched condition of the poor economies is due above all to historical reasons: colonialism and, in the post-colonial era, the constraints to independent development imposed by the hegemonic influence of the rich industrial states. The waste of scarce resources by international and civil wars, and the dictatorships with their upper class luxury consumption and inefficient, thus development – obstructing exploitation structures—often supported by the industrialised nations-have for a long time repressed and in many cases destroyed autonomous development potential. The colonial and post-colonial distortion also contributed at least indirectly to the current population problems of the poor countries. The politically inflicted mass poverty and under-development stabilised or in fact brought about economic, socio-psychological and ideological mechanisms which oppose an effective population policy. As we know, the average educational level in many developing countries, especially among women, is too low to give a modern population policy a chance of success. Mass unemployment in the poor countries is the result of poverty. In this respect, it is about a production-side problem: too few resources, too little real and human capital, and the inefficient, unproductive use of much of the anyway limited added value of society. The picture is totally different in the rich countries—the over-production economies.

Unemployment in Over-Production Systems

The main cause of mass unemployment in the industrialised nations has nothing to do with shortages. It is a phenomenon of surplus. Greater possibilities of production can no longer be used 'sufficiently' profitably because the required demand is lacking. Production is done for profit. The necessary collateral condition is the satisfying of consumer needs. Employment is not even such a condition, but only a side effect which lapses immediately when labour-free production is technically possible. Thus, national income must be shared among wages and profits (or income from property). Profit is the difference between earnings and costs.

Earnings depend upon demand. Macroeconomic costs consist mainly of wages and salaries (including social security contributions). These definitive connections mean that profit can be made only if overall demand is greater than the total cost of labour. But in the final analysis this demand can only come from the profit-earners themselves. In his book, A *Treatise on Money*, Keynes described this nexus as the theory of the Widow's cruse. Under capitalistic conditions, labour is only sought or hired if profit can be earned with it. But as making a profit depends upon the demand for consumption and investment by the shareholders, it can be seen that the degree of employment is determined by the demand behaviour of the class that receives income from property. In this respect, the widespread belief that greater investment also leads to more employment, namely via the effect of investment in demand, is right.

Lower Wages Mean Lower Demand

The lower the level of wages, and given an unchanged total demand, the greater are the profits that can be made. But it is more likely that in the case of falling wages the overall demand will also drop. For stabilising total demand would require the recipients of income from property to increase their spending on consumption and/or investment to the degree to which wages and the consumption based on them fell.

During the last 10 to 15 years the development of profits in most industrialised nations has been very favourable. But profits would have grown more strongly if the demand of the shareholders had been much greater. This would have created more employment at the same time. Thus, it can be assumed that the profits are simply too high for the shareholders to be able to go in for meaningful consumption or make profitable investments. That is the reason for the extreme redirection of capital from fixed assets to portfolio investment. The growth of speculative (unproductive) financial transactions during the 1980s and 1990s (buzzword: casino capitalism), corresponded with a relatively weak formation of real capital.

Wage rises, of course, narrow the scope for profit. But precisely this effect stimulated efforts to improve the profit situation not only by investment in rationalisation, but also by investment in expansion aimed at the growing mass purchasing power. Since more is being invested, the profit mass also is growing according to the principle of the Widow's cruse. Too low wages, as it were, relieve the shareholders of the pressure to innovate and invest and allow them to earn their profits too easily. That is the real message of the 'purchasing power theory' of wages.

Over-Accumulation and Under-Consumption

Overproduction has two different causes which, however, mostly occur in tandem. They are over-investment, or creation of over-capacities, on the one hand, and lack of demand due to relative saturation and an absence of mass purchasing power on the other. But the main reason for mass unemployment in the rich hemisphere currently lies on the demand side. During the first three decades after the Second World War supply and demand rose in relative balance.

Economic fluctuations showed up as temporary declines in generally positive GDP growth rates. These decades of (dynamic) balance of growth are often described today as the era of 'Fordism'. Its essential feature is that rising wages ensure continuing growth of consumption, so that equally growing profits also flow relatively continuously into investments to expand capacity and create jobs. The label 'Fordism' expresses the 'simple' view of the theory of the buying power of wages which is said to have been propagated by Henry Ford I. This was that his workers should earn enough to be able to buy the cars they made.

The astonishingly balanced development of supply and demand from 1950 to the mid-1970s was due above all to post-war reconstruction and the pent-up demand of consumers who were starved by wartime economy shortages. This stimulated positive investment sentiment, and high investments brought at the same time high profits. The post-war growth that led within a short time to full employment was also linked with growth in productivity which on multi-year average was more than twice that of the crisis period of the last 25 years. Thus, the so-called employment threshold (the GDP growth rate point at which employment growth begins) was much higher in those days than it is now, although there was full employment over a longer period. This simple fact opposes the thesis often propounded today that mass unemployment is above all related to rationalisation. It is not rationalisation per se, that is, progress that boosts productivity, which is the evil. The problem is that the mistakes in distribution policy which are rooted in capitalistic structures result in increases in supply encountering insufficient demand for goods, whereby the demand for labour drops. However, the fact that demand policy contradicts the requirements of a social ethic that is ecologically responsible and right for the interests of the poor countries was already spelled out. So if a demand-oriented growth policy is practised at all, it should be designed to be as environmentally compatible as possible. After all, there are possibilities for that, such as by expanding the production of services that spare resources. A one-hour driving lesson costs more energy than one hour of ballet instruction.

The politically initiated and implemented over-liberalisation and surrender of social prosperity to global competition since the 1970s, which reproduces the old self-destructive mechanism of laissez faire, have during the last two decades markedly accelerated the crisis development inherent in the system.

Summing Up, it is Noted that

- full employment in the rich economies would certainly be possible by means of demand policy, but only at a high cost to the environment that is concomitant with high growth rates;
- the growth policy of the rich countries impairs the poor economics' possibilities of medium to long-term growth, since these are falling back ever further in the competition for ever scarcer and thus ever more expensive resources;
- the environmental collapse currently expected for the third or fourth generation after us, which obviously also will trigger a collapse of the world economy and –probably ahead of that –armed conflicts which today are hardly imaginable, would happen very much

sooner if economic growth were to be increased to such a degree that it would bring full employment worldwide;

- in the long term, the problem of global unemployment and global poverty can only be solved by a policy of massive redistribution, and in fact a redistribution of work and income, whereby increases in productivity must be used mainly or only for shortening working hours. That is a demand which appears to be utopian. But utopias of today often have the quality of scripting the reality of tomorrow.

Chapter—4

For Richer, For Fairer

Poverty Reduction and Income Distribution

Will the international target of reducing poverty by half over the next 15 years be met? Not unless growth efforts are accompanied by significant improvements in income distribution,. Poverty reduction is a twin function of the rate of growth and of changes in income distribution. The research shows better distribution has as much impact on reducing poverty as had increased growth. And given predicted rates of economic growth, it emerges as the factor that will make the main difference between success and failure for new 'pro-poor' growth strategies.

Over the past decade, the amount of poverty reduction resulting from a given rate of economic growth has varied in close step with income distribution. On average, a growth rate of 10 per cent reduced the poverty headcount (the percentage of people living on less that $ 1 a day) by 9 per cent in countries where income was fairly equally distributed. However in countries where income was unequally distributed, a growth rate of 10 per cent reduced the poverty headcount by only 3 per cent.

The World Bank estimates that developing countries will grow at 4 per cent per capita per annum until 2015. So the good news is that the income-poverty target is attainable provided that significant improvements take place in income distribution. These can be achieved ex-ante, by designing growth strategies that increase disproportionately the incomes of the poorest, or ex-post, by redistributing income through taxation. Many questions arise. What is the recipe for income-redistributing growth? Is there a trade-off between growth and distribution? An ex-post strategies of reduction feasible? These questions are far from new. Indeed, to a large degree, they are the very questions on which the development studies profession is founded. Nevertheless, they have been neglected in recent years. Does current research offer new perspectives? Articles in this issue of insights offer six main conclusions. They are that:

- We need a way to measure 'pro-poor growth'. The concept originates from the 1990 World Development Report of the World Bank and is taken to mean a labour intensive growth path that encompasses the economic activities of the poor. However, such a growth path could be accompanied by increasing, declining or static income inequality. McCulloch and Baulch propose that the 'poverty bias of growth' or PBG (whether pro-poor or not) be defined by comparing actual change in income distribution with the change that would have resulted had all incomes grown at one rate with no change to income inequality. This difference is compared in their report (opposite) for two states in India. From this comparison it emerges that growth in Bihar State was accompanied by worsening income distribution and has been biased against the poor, whereas in Andhra Pradesh the reverse was true.

- Growth might be expected to be pro-poor if it takes place in areas and sectors where the poor live and work. For the poorest countries this means mostly in rural areas and to a large extent in agriculture. In Asia, Green Revolution technologies were adopted by poor farmers because they were scale-neutral and low-risk. Poor non-farmers also benefited from the extra employment and lower food prices that resulted. In Sub-Saharan Africa, the Green Revolution has been slower in coming, but research at Reading by Mosley suggests an African Green Revolution will help. In Uganda, for example, the spread of new technologies in maize and cassava has contributed to sharp falls in poverty, notable in the country's North, where mosaic-resistant cassava has made a conspicuous difference to farmer's yields and incomes in an otherwise poor and undeveloped region.

- Even so, as many will remember well from debates about the Green Revolution in Asia, not everybody benefits from growth. In Ethiopia, researchers from the Universities of Oxford and Addis Ababa found that rural poverty has fallen sharply since the change of government in 1992, driven by market liberalisation and better weather (see Dercon, backfold). Yet those who have gained have been those with assets, including land, oxen for ploughing, education and access to public goods such as roads. Those without assets are left behind. Rural inequality has actually risen, implying Ethiopia could reduce poverty faster if policies countered inequality yet maintained current growth rates.

- People without assets might be expected to compensate by migrating or moving out of agriculture. Sometimes this happens, but seeking off-farm opportunities may be easier for the haves than the have-nots. In rural Zimbabwe, for example, Piesse and Thirtle have shown that (in more remote areas at least) those with higher farm incomes are better placed to exploit off-farm opportunities, including the option of working in town.

- In any case, migration to town may not offer much to the unskilled—again, a problem facing those without assets. The evidence here comes from China, in research carried out by the Institute of Economics and Statistics. Wage employment has increased in urban China, but wage inequality has increased sharply, with falling real wages for the unskilled.

- The efficiency (hence the growth) and equity trade-off is far from clear cut. Analysis by Knight of the reasons behind rising wage-income inequality in China has revealed that some of these changes reflect greater labour market efficiency. In other words, more productive, experienced and skilled workers have become better paid. Other changes hint at new inefficiencies creeping into China's labour market, such as growing labour market, such as growing discrimination: females and minority groups find they are disadvantaged in the labour market, whereas members of the Communist Party are more likely to get jobs. Other signs are sharper segmentation, with state employees paid more than private sector counterparts and growing differences in wage rates between the provinces, not offset by labour mobility.

The cross-section of findings offered in these pages does not amount to a systematic review of the 'inequality question' in developing countries. Far from it: here is fertile ground for further research. Even so, we are confident that it is time to promote inequality to the fore of the research and policy agenda.

Chapter—5
City Politics
A Voice for the Poor

By 2020 the world's urban population will rise by almost 1.5 billion. Cities and towns house a growing proportion of poor people, partly because of the increased share of urban population of the total but also because economic recession and adjustment policies often hit poorer urban residents the hardest. Cities are associated with economic growth and wealth generation and yet inequality is high. Poor people generally live in substandard conditions, may not benefit from job creation, and suffer high levels of pollution, crime and violence.

How can city governments cope with the challenges of population growth and increased global economic competition, and meet the needs of poor residents/is urban governance responsive to the needs of the poor? Are the agencies responsible for city government, especially the municipalities, addressing poor people's needs? Are NGOs and people's organisations playing a greater role in service delivery? Or is their role one of advocacy and lobbying? If so, how do they relate to the formal political system? Can governments fulfil their responsibilities, including poverty reduction? How can the well-being of poor urban governance institutions prioritise their needs? In assessing the responsiveness of city government to poor people, three key questions are addressed:

How can the poor influence the agenda of the institutions of urban governance?

The influence of poor residents on decision making is controlled, in part, by the formal political system.

Democratisation gives people a vote. However, this vote means more when elected representatives depend on the political support of poor people—where they are a majority, or are well organised, or where there is a ward-based system. If poor people are organised enough, to articulate their needs and demand a fair share of urban resources, NGOs can help poor groups organise better and provide support for networking.

Where poor people are not organised it does not mean they are politically powerless. Poor people in this situation, however, are prey to the disadvantages of patronage and unlikely to be included in formal consultative processes. For an electoral system to be truly responsive, specific mechanisms and channels, such as consultative and participatory processes at city and sub-city levels, are needed to complement representative democracy. Although, these channels do not necessarily include the poorest or make a marked difference to resource allocation pro-poor decisions are unlikely without them.

How can cities finance their activities and reduce poverty?

Democratisation has not, in many countries, brought allocation of financial resources or the revenue-raising capacity for local governments to fulfil their responsibilities. The responsiveness of city governments to poor people's needs thus depends, on whose voices are heard in the arenas of political decision making. Responsiveness also depends on how available financial resources are allocated and how the programmes they finance are designed. There is scope, for city governments to increase property and business revenues, and to borrow for capital investment. Whether increased financial resources benefit poor people depends on how the demands of external investors and creditors are reconciled with the demands of poor residents; the willingness of politicians and officials to address the distributive implications of existing and planned spending; and efficient transparent financial management. If funds are made available to sub-city levels of government or if expenditure can be influenced by ward councillors, the funds might then be used to meet the priorities of poor residents

What are the necessities of urban living and how can access to then be ensured?

An adequate income: Work opportunities should be the top priority. City governments can, however, support the urban economy in general and the economic activities of the poor in particular. Firstly they can ensure that the basic services are efficiently provided. Secondly city governments can refrain from activities that destroy the assets and livelihoods of the poor, especially eviction of informal settlements and micro-enterprises. Savings and credit schemes can be more appropriately organised at a community level and supported by NGOs.

Land ownership is a common aspiration for poor households. A home with secure tenure (not necessarily title) provides security, an appreciating asset, access to services, and a base for economic activities. Increasing the opportunities for poor households to gain access to a well-located plot of land is an important component of any poverty reduction strategy. Many never fulfil their dream and the needs of those who cannot, or do not wish to become home-owners should not be neglected, however.

Local government is potentially more responsive to poor residents than are central government agencies, although this depends on the balance of political power and bureaucratic perceptions. The limited ability of the public sector to secure benefits for the poor from public-private partnerships in land development, suggests that more informal arrangements and the involvement of CSOs may be better ways forward.

Environmental Services: Land alone will not reduce poverty but must be linked to a healthy living environment—a package of appropriate and affordable environmental services, such as public transport, water and sanitation, solid waste collection, and energy for cooking and lighting. Rather than discussing appropriate standards, detailed issues of financing and affordability or how continued provision can be assured for each of these services, the research focused on how far decision making channels, mechanisms, and partnership arrangements ensure that providers are responsive to the needs and priorities of poor residents.

Collaborative planning and decision-making arrangements are one promising alternative, despite the current shortcomings of participatory budgeting, for responsiveness to the poor to be built in to such processes, local bureaucrats need to change their attitudes and working practices. Is it possible and acceptable for poor people to have to rely on their own resources their households and networks—resources that are very limited? Informal networks and links can, however, provide mutual support and access to politicians and bureaucrats, community associations though not always present, inclusive or transparent, can play an important role in articulating poor residents' views and in organising self-help activities. There is scope for formal representative community organisations, for informal links between people's organisations and the power structures, and for networking between people's groups. NGOs can play an important role in developing the capacity of community organisations and in facilitating networking. Where NGOs play a role in service delivery. However, there is a danger that the resulting close relationship with local government detracts from their ability to empower poor people and challenge inappropriate policies. City governments, it is clear, cannot cope with the challenges of population and economic growth and respond to the needs of poor people alone. Only in alliance with other actors is there some hope that poverty can be overcome. For CSOs, many of which were forged during struggles for democratisation, this implies moving beyond confrontation to engagement. To form alliances between CSOs and city governments that put the interests of the poor first, poor people must be able to exercise their political rights.

Chapter—6

Tapping the Market

Can Private Enterprise Supply Water to the Poor?

Over 170 million people have no access to clean water in urban areas throughout the world. Inefficient operation of state-owned water companies is at the root of this injustice: gross over-staffing and political interference in tariff-setting have starved utilities of the resources needed to expand piped networks to impoverished areas.

The failure of the supply-driven approach has led to public private partnerships (PPPs) designed to shift water utilities towards a demand-driven approach. Have these changes been accompanied by improved access to clean, affordable water for the urban poor? Has PPP improved equity in urban water supply? Are the new private sector operators addressing the needs of the urban poor in practice? This article examines the extent to which the urban poor have benefited or not from this newly emerging institutional arrangement.

The 'public' approach typically provides unclean water sporadically. It requires expensive, highly educated professionals, significant subsidies and tends to service clients on high and middle incomes whilst charging low tariffs. International financial institutions have failed to enable the public water suppliers to improve performance, either through massive investment in engineering, or through capacity building and institutional development.

At the other extreme is an efficient, demand driven, customer-oriented approach, the 'small scale independent providers', delivering water to cities' inhabitants, with near 100 per cent bill collection efficiency. Promoting local employment and servicing the poor, this approach has, until recently, been ignored by water sector professionals. Lacking regulatory oversight, however, their prices are typically 10 to 20 times higher than those paid by high-income consumers connected to the network. Which of these providers are most effective at serving the poor? The starting point is to recognise the evidence suggesting that the urban poor are prepared to pay to meet their survival and convenience needs for water.

Notwithstanding the rhetoric to the contrary by some trade unions and NGOs, initial results from larger cities indicate that the efficiency of 'privatised' water utilities has improved markedly: leakages are down and net revenue is up through improved billing and collection and reduction in personnel. Whether this is due to the alleged benefits to private sector investment or the freedom of foreign operators to manage without being beholden to employee and entrenched political interests is not yet clear.

Has the extension of the network to poor communities been speeded up?

Concession contracts require private operators to meet coverage targets. But the decisions on the direction of network expansion to meet targets are usually left to the operators as regulatory bodies are usually formed after contract signing. So are poor communities given priority? Technical criteria based on cost-effectiveness in the construction of main pipes, commercial criteria based on pressure from property developers, and political criteria based on vote-winning tactics may all conflict with social criteria based on the pressing needs of poor communities.

Is the cost of household connection affordable by the poor?

Even where operators do give priority to extending the piped network into poor communities, difficult issues arise over the financing of secondary pipelines, household connections and meter installation. Techniques are evolving to reduce the cost of connection so as to ensure affordable for all. These may take the form of tripartite arrangements whereby the public sector provides grants for the purchase of materials, community groups provide voluntary labour, and the private operator provides technical assistance. NGOs may contribute by providing crucial skills in team management and local understanding not usually found in the bureaucratic culture of public sector institutions or the techno-professional culture of private water companies.

Is the water tariff affordable by the poor?

Even where poor communities have been connected, there is no assurance that householders can afford the water charges. Many have no job security or regular income. Billing arrangements need to be shortened from the monthly norm to fit the short-term financial horizon imposed by household poverty.

Property-based tariff structures still discriminate against the poor by providing far cheaper water per litre for high-income households consuming large volumes for swimming pools and sprinkler systems. Reforms should positively discriminate in favour of the poor, with some cross-subsidisation from richer to poorer households. However, where the initial life-line block is greater than average monthly domestic water use by the poor (perhaps over $6m^3$ per household a month), middle income groups benefit the most. A single volumetric tariff for domestic consumers with subsidies aimed at facilitating water connections rather than consumption is now being recommended.

This article focuses on the three major challenges for the sector in the new millennium.

- First it is crucial to develop regulatory skills to oversee this affordable expansion. The key capacity constraints facing municipalities—usually the public sector partners in PPPs.
- Second is the need to incorporate the skills of small-scale independent providers
- Thirdly it is important to move beyond the metropolitan capitals, to where cross-subsidies are more achievable, and address the water needs of the urban poor in the myriad of secondary towns in the south.

Chapter—7

Democracy and Poverty:

Are They Interlinked?

Democracy assistance and poverty reduction are rightly becoming two focal—and related—issues for development assistance. Increasingly, many organizations, including intergovernmental, national and civil society, are focusing their work on these two areas. Furthermore, the relationship between these two issues is complex and ever changing. There is thus a need to develop methodologies for linking democracy assistance and poverty reduction at both the policy and programme levels. International IDEA (Institute for Democracy and Electoral Assistance) in cooperation with the World Bank and the United Nations Development Programme, is developing concrete strategies that address these two objectives in a mutually reinforcing way. Through an overall situation analysis followed by regional meetings in sub-Saharan Africa, South Asia, Latin America, the Caucasus and the Arab region, the Institute has marshalled evidence of some of the key problems that affect democracy consolidation and poverty reduction in these countries:

- Corruption and its undermining effect on popular confidence in public institutions.
- Continuing economic instability coupled with the lack of strategies for addressing the twin challenges of poverty and increasing popular participation in its alleviation.
- The extremely limited nature of citizen's influence on overall policy and decision-making processes despite the spread of formal democratic institutions.

- A trend in many post-communist states towards viewing growing poverty as a direct consequence of a transition to democracy.

In short, the evidence is not very encouraging for the prospects for democracy consolidation and poverty reduction. The critical step International IDEA advocates is the development of an approach that not only seeks to put democracy assistance and poverty reduction on top of the development assistance agenda, but also to encourage all involved to treat them as twin elements of an integrated programme of action.

Through a focus on accountable governance, promotion and protection of citizenship and rights and increased popular participation, International IDEA believes that both democracy and poverty reduction can be addressed simultaneously. Policy recommendations are being developed and will be shared in the course of this year with governments, international organizations and civil society bodies.

International IDEA believes that democracy promotion can be used as a tool for fulfilling a variety of objectives. Democracy matters because it protects human rights and preserves human dignity. But democracy also matters because it helps to address some of the most critical challenges facing states today: peace, development, economic growth and stability.

Democracy does not guarantee any one of these, but increasingly it seems to be a precondition for them in the long term. Thus, advocating democracy goes beyond being a moral issue; it becomes *fundamental* to advancing the well-being of people and the stability of states. International IDEA will continue to explore the link between democracy and the major issues facing society today—and continue to argue the case for democracy.

Chapter—8

Taking a Lead in the Fight Against Poverty?

World Bank and IMF Speed Implementation of their New Strategy

A change in development policy strategy in the poorest countries is at present being prepared with incredible speed. The IMF-style structural adjustment programmes that have been criticised for many years are being scrapped. The countries are now to take their own decisions on their paths to development. Their governments will no longer formulate poverty reduction programmes top-down, but in an intensive and long-term dialogue with societal groups and organisations. Governments and institutions of the North commit themselves to supporting these processes, such as by debt relief on an unprecedented scale. Dream or reality?

New Strategy Paper

Behind this euphoria lies a new abbreviation, PRSP, standing for Poverty Reduction Strategy Paper, which the IMF and World Bank invented last year. The G-7 countries in Cologne not only announced debt relief for the Heavily Indebted Poor Countries (HIPCs) but also demanded that it must serve above all for poverty reduction. The PRSP concept was then presented at the annual conference of the two Bretton Woods organisations

The most important principles of the new "super weapon" in the fight against poverty are:

- PRSPs are papers, which describe the medium-term development paths of the poorest countries of the South, particularly their strategies to combat poverty, and by this means enlist international support. A PRSP is not only the prerequisite for granting debt forgiveness in the context of the HIPC initiative. It is also necessary for all new IMF and World Bank loans to the so-called IDA countries, the some 70 poorest countries that receive concessional loans from the World Bank's International Development Agency (IDA). According to the World Bank, PRSPs should also be required for all future pledges of bilateral development assistance.

- Not only social sector programmes, but also the economic and financial policies of the developing countries are in future to be aimed at fighting poverty. Previously, the IMF always pronounced that a growth-oriented national economy and a far-reaching integration in the world market would have a trickle-down effect and also benefit the poor. Now the poor are to be asked what policies can help materially to improve their situation.
- PRSPs are to be developed on the basis of self-responsible country ownership. Accordingly, development and structural adjustment strategies are no longer to be developed by the Washington finance institutions, but the countries themselves.
- The heading "country ownership" is to underline that not only governments are called upon, PRSPs should come into being in a participatory process. That means involvement of trade unions, NGOs, cooperatives, associations, grass roots, groups, political parties and parliaments. A country's PRSP should be developed in a societal debate, a dialogue between governments on one side and parliamentary, private sector and civil society on the other.

Rhetoric or Reality?

Are PRSPs the expression of a change of paradigm? In brief, if all what the papers contain is implemented in a consistent and wide ranging, way, the chances of achieving it are good but there are a number of open questions. The answers to them will have a bearing on success or failure.

- Is the IMF really changing its policy on the poorest countries or merely wrapping its old policy in new words? The growing criticism of the IMF in recent years strengthened latterly by the evaluation of the ESAF (Enhanced Structural Adjustment Facility) programmes, which once again proved their blatant weaknesses called for reaction and is now triggering changes—real or only rhetorical? There will be no more old-style ESAF loans based on macroeconomic structural adjustment programmes. But the credit line remains, and is now called the Poverty Reduction and Growth Facility (PRGF). This will be granted on the basis of the PRSPs, which in each case must also be accepted by the IMF board of directors. How much influence will the IMF have on the design of the PRSPS? What happens if a government choose macroeconomic strategies combat poverty which go against previous IMF policy? Open questions. Moreover, there is still no answer to the question of why the IMF is at all coming on with long-term and low-interest lines of credit in the poorest countries.

Mixed Feelings with Regard to World Bank Role

- Will the World Bank use the PRSP process to expand its own institutional power further? NGOs in the North and South are viewing this with mixed feelings. Many welcome the fact that for the moment the World Bank appears to be asserting itself against its twin, the IMF. On the other hand, 50 years of experience with World Bank strategies have certainly not strengthened their trust in the Bank's ability to make a convincing fight against poverty. That is why the EURODAD network also questions the role of the World Bank (and the IMF) in the PRSP process. It says the papers should not be presented to the two financial institutions, whose power over the development strategies of countries of the South thus would increase further. Rather, PRSPs should for example, be laid before a Round Table of all donors chaired by the United Nations Development Programme (UNDP).

Ownership

- The principles of developing countries being responsible for their own development strategies are as old as it is – in theory—right. There have been frequent complaints about shortcomings in ownership. But now, after decades of development strategies being set and structural adjustment programmes being dictated from outside, the governments of the poorest countries, which in many cases have only weak institutional capacities, can hardly be taken on sole responsibility overnight. In addition, of course, not a few of the countries are ruled by corrupt political elites (promoted from outside over decades) that give little reason to hope they would immediately switch to poverty reduction politics. Scepticism and critical observation is justified even if there is no alternative to governments of the south taking over greater responsibility.
- Civil society actors are now asked to help out in particular in those countries whose governments appear to be less trustworthy. A nice idea that has little to do with real life. Civil society actors in developing countries in general and in the poorest countries in particular are extraordinarily weak institutions which in many cases are totally dependent on financing from the North.

The civil society landscape in other countries is even weaker. However, social actors in many countries could make useful contributions to developing sustainable strategies. But that calls for meaningful and lasting support, including financial support, capacity-building, and in some countries also political pressure to gain scope for societal engagement.

It is reasonable that not only the World Bank and other official donors but also, and above all, the northern NGO partners of these actors are now giving much thought to how civil societies in the south can be strengthened.

Participation?

Even assuming there were civil society actors capable of dialogue, that does not clarify what participation in the PRSP process is really supposed to mean. Is civil society only to be listened to, or an it if necessary refuse to approve a PRSP? What impact would a refusal have on acceptance of the document by the IMF and World Bank and other donor? And in view of the great time pressure, will civil society be at all able to formulate, discuss and feed their positions into the process? It could be of decisive importance for the current debate on the PRSP model to delink the urgently needed debt relief from drawing up a PRSP programme, which simply needs more time. For example, it is conceivable that there would be no great problems in granting a country a moratorium on debt servicing so long as a PRSP process is continuing and then for giving debt when it is completed. That would ease the time problem for NGOs and at the same time maintain pressure on governments actually to arrive at poverty reduction strategies that were developed in a participatory process.

Other Causes of Poverty in Developing Countries

The entire current process is focused on the countries of the south, their governments and societies. That diverts attention from the responsibility of the donors and creditors. Not only that the IMF's structural adjustment programmes to date have been counterproductive for fighting poverty (why does the IMF not admit that openly just for once?). Not only that the now promised debt reliefs are coming much too late (the debt crisis of the poorest countries was deplored decades ago!). The present strategy also ignores various other exogenous causes of poverty in the South. What impacts do the finance and trade policies of northern countries have on the modest attempts to enable sustainable development in the South? What consequences will the continuing cutting of development budgets have on the South (no one anyway ventures to talk nowadays about the old 0.7 per cent ODA-GNP ratio)? For the donors and creditors to now pass the buck of sole responsibility to the governments of the South and present themselves in the background as noble do-gooders may be a successful strategy in terms of domestic politics, but not an acceptable one for development policy.

Chapter—9

Land Tenure

Securing Land for the Urban Poor

Around the world, especially in Asia and Africa, towns and cities are expanding rapidly. For the poorest people, finding affordable, safe and secure urban land for shelter has become increasingly difficult. This is because:

- Overall competition for land makes it increasingly costly;
- Central urban areas are being developed for commercial use;
- Natural features such as mountains or swamps limit physical urban expansion; and
- Meeting land management and planning standards (concerned with legality, technical and administrative accuracy) is expensive.

As a result, a large and increasing proportion of urban populations are forced to live in peripheral areas or occupy marginalised and dangerous locations. These settlements are often illegal, and providing inadequate shelter and lacking essential services, only exacerbate the problems of the poor. Higher levels of ill-health, unemployment and non-sustainable land-use often result. Furthermore, residents may also be under constant threat of eviction by government, and exploitation by landowners.

Experience shows that, if residents in such areas feel secure and safe from eviction, they do over time improve their neighbourhoods. Recognition of and granting of secure forms of tenure to previously illegal settlements often provides the incentive to communities to invest their resources in upgrading their housing and wider neighbourhoods. Security of tenure also brings the improved likelihood of basic infrastructure and other essential community services.

There is a wide range of urban land tenure systems. In many urban areas, including areas designated illegal by government, there are informal or customary tenure systems—these are often the commonest form of tenure and are expanding most rapidly.

While statutory or "legal" forms of tenure (for example freehold or leasehold agreements) offer many advantages, such as full individual rights and security and access to formal credit systems, they can also cause the very problems they were intended to solve:

- Higher rental levels, which may displace existing renters;
- The selling out of the secure land to higher income groups
- Encouragement of new illegal/informal settlements, as the poorest hope that they will also eventually get security of tenure;
- Encouragement of landowners and developers to hold land, without investing in its improvement or paying taxes on its increased value—which serves to attract even greater levels of investment and land price inflation.

In addition, if people's incomes remain low and the capacity of the banks or credit unions is weak, statutory forms of tenure alone may not necessarily stimulate neighbourhood improvements

Consequently, careful analysis of existing systems of informal and customary tenure and property rights is required, before embarking on major land management and tenure reforms. These can provide both acceptable levels of security and access to credit, which in turn stimulate improvements to local neighbourhoods. Before any decisions are made, tenure policies must recognise the likely impact on tenants, the poor and other vulnerable groups, especially women.

For these reasons, it is sometimes better to increase the rights of residents (e.g. by protecting them from the threat of forced evictions, or by increasing their access to essential utilities or credit), rather than assuming that they need freehold or leasehold titles.

Strategies for providing shelter now recognise the diverse nature of needs, and the positive contribution which decent housing makes to social and economic development at both national and local levels. They also recognise that the most effective way of mobilising the resources required is to encourage investment in housing by individuals, communities and the private sector.

Recent experience shows that many governments are now introducing positive approaches which are market-sensitive and encourage more efficient use of available land. These include measures to encourage landowners and developers to allocate a specified proportion of units to low-income groups out of profits generated from planning permission granted by (and therefore partly created by) the government. Public-private partnerships and revisions to planning standards and administrative procedures have also demonstrated that it is possible to reduce the costs of access to land for the poor even under conditions of market-led development, thus reducing urban sprawl, the occurrence of slum settlements and levels of poverty.

Chapter—10

Social Development

The Way Forward

The idea of development is seductive; it is also elusive. It promises a lot to everyone, but it has failed to deliver to those in greatest need. In 1944 development and economic growth were largely synonymous, but by the 1950s, when it became clear that this model was not helping the poor, a focus on social development evolved. Its advocates argued that economic growth as development should be pursued, but complemented with social development programmes for those who were "excluded." This approach did not fare much better, and the idea of socio-economic development, in which social development principles were to be mainstreamed in the economic growth process, was born.

Social development is commonly used to include the policies and programmes designed to combat poverty, unemployment, crime, social exclusion, ill-health and illiteracy—all noble causes. But noble intentions do not easily produce the desired results; they sometimes produce the opposite. Most social development programmes, in both developed and developing countries, run the risk of fostering the victim mentality, creating dependency and deepening disepowerment, although they seek the reverse.

The 1995 Social Summit in Copenhagen, which addressed the themes of poverty, unemployment and social exclusion, was a significant milestone in the history of development. Apart from its direct outcomes in the form of commitments and an action plan adopted by well over 100 heads of state, the summit raised the political profile of social development. But five years later, while several developing countries managed real improvements in their social development indicators, the problems identified at Copenhagen are still with us and many have worsened. The main reasons for this are the usual one—lack of new and additional resources and lack of political will.

The results of the Social Summit review will be presented at the Special Session of the United Nations General Assembly in Geneva shortly. Hopefully, the Special Session will generate not only innovative solutions, but also the political will to carry them out. The General Assembly three simple and somewhat basic recommendations should be kept in mind:

- Reiterate poverty eradication as the top priority of the international and national development agenda.
- Recommend an operationally enhanced human development strategy as the practical framework for development cooperation for poverty eradication.
- Encourage development agencies and governments to use their existing sectoral mandates as entry points in a synergistic framework provided by the operationally enhanced human development framework, which could also be called a sustainable livelihoods approach.

All of the above are politically and operationally feasible. The implication of the first is to focus on the single theme of poverty eradication for action over the next five years. Social exclusion could be addressed in the strategy for poverty reduction, and employment should be seen as one of the entry points for action in the strategic action framework for poverty eradication. This provides a clear agenda around which political will, resources and action can be mobilized.

The second and third proposals addressed the weaknesses of the welfare and/or growth and trickle down approaches to poverty eradication in current vogue. Such a social agenda creates a no-win situation, in the sense that even when it succeeds in squeezing out some reprieve for workers, the poor and the disadvantaged, it produces more victims waiting to be saved and so fosters a pervasive disempowerment process. Further, and more importantly, the rationale places the economy before people.

The human development approach offers a powerful and viable alternative by fundamentally reversing the premise on which development planning proceeds—to put the economy at the service of the people rather than the reverse. The question then is how to address the social development agenda through an enhanced human development approach?

At the operational level, the following would greatly enhance the human development approach to poverty eradication:

- Begin by focusing on what people have (the assets approach), not what they need by defining assets broadly to include human, social, national and physical capital.
- Understand people's adaptive strategies to shocks and stresses and seek to further develop and release their creativity by appropriate policy, governance, technology and investment shifts and inputs.
- Mainstream the environment by giving natural capital the same level of importance as human, social and physical capital in the programme design framework.
- Mainstream gender by paying attention to different patterns of asset ownership by men and women and their different adaptive strategies.

On an optimistic note, the evolution of development practice has more often than not been characterized by a willingness to learn from past mistakes and to move forward with new and innovative paradigms. This spirit must continue if the dream of a poverty-free world is to be realized.

Chapter—11

NGOs

Searching for Solid Ground

The role of NGOs should be to foster the emergence of a world-wide civil society. The first step towards making globalization a more democratic affair. NGOs were not born yesterday, but the rising number of conflicts that have reverberated in recent decades around a world globalized in the neoliberal mould has led them to multiply and diversify into highly visible bodies.

Who are the main players in this process of globalization? Governments (politics) and the market (the economy) are the twin pillars supporting the productive systems and structures of modern societies. So who has the legitimate right to change them? The societies themselves, for they alone are made up of citizens grouped together as a people, a nation or a country. The right does not belong to governments, state structures, corporate executives or markets. This is why, as NGOs, our attention is directed at civil society itself.

At the global level, our basic task is to foster the emergence of a worldwide civil society as a precondition to calling for a new style of globalization: "world governance." Our mission is to encourage the re-founding of globalization along more democratic lines by taking part in public debate and promulgating the concept of world citizenship. The political stances we take and our lobbying activities, therefore, do not come out of the blue, but are efforts to transmit the main currents and aspirations of public opinion and make this opinion stronger and clearer.

The Tripartite Mirage

All NGO actions are based on an obvious priority, namely,

that of supporting social protests and public pressure during major negotiations taking place within the main circles of power. That is why the agreements we conclude and the alliances we forge are above all else aimed at organizations and movements arising from civil society. That is also why we build forums, coalitions and networks that straddle national borders. On the basis of our approach, we can think globally, set up links between the particular and the universal, swap experiences and keep ourselves regularly informed.

Today, global power is monopolized by major multilateral organizations, and is fundamentally anti-democratic in its structure and workings. In their current form, these organizations' claims to embody democracy and universal citizenship ring hollow. In fact, their only possible claim to legitimacy is through the vote. But not all the national governments represented in international organizations have been elected by popular suffrage, and very few of them represent all the different social forces that go into making up their nations.

Does this mean that NGOs, which are supposed to embody civil society, should claim to represent these peoples? Does it mean that our goal should be to win a place at the heart of a future new world democratic order? Does it mean that we are fully entitled to a seat in some new tripartite structure—made up of government, companies and civil society—that some people are campaigning for? In my opinion, all of that is just a mirage; even worse, we risk losing sight of our most useful and most legitimate purpose if we embrace that vision.

Small Players, Big Issues

NGOs are not out to conquer power or win elections, be they world, national or local bodies. We are not set up like political parties, even though our activities are public and seem highly politicized. We cannot even present ourselves as representatives of civil society because civil society has not entrusted us with any such mandate.

So what do we want? To reach out, mobilize, educate, get across messages, suggest, innovate, persuade and politically strengthen various groups in civil society and, more specifically, those excluded from the decision-making process. We want to give a voice to ideas, values, questions and proposals that involve social justice, a more equitable distribution of wealth, respect for the environment, the struggle against poverty and social exclusion.

Who are we? Small players, compared to the other pillars of civil society, such as trade unions and professional organizations, or bodies in the state or the market. But we are also—and this is something new—"big" players, because our mission and our field of action are not limited to a given society, national economy or single government. Our task is to form a bridge between the local and the global: in other words, to deal with what is universal, with what is common to all humanity. Human rights, social crises and environmental protection are global issues. We deal with them in specific situations, but our perspective is always planetary.

So where does our legitimacy lie? In the quality of the values, principles and ideals we defend. In the relevance and the importance of the issues we raise. In the inventiveness of the proposals we put forward. Our only source of legitimacy is our ability to develop ideas aimed at action—ideas that are up to the standards of public duty to which we aspire.

Chapter—12

What was Wrong with Structural Adjustment

In Defence of a Much-Maligned Strategy

After decades of stranded development theories, ideologies and paradigms, "structural adjustment", with its demands for clean fiscal policy and an end to uneconomic state enterprises, political privileges, market and exchange rate intervention and corruption, entered the aid arena like a refreshing dawn after a long night of frustrating dreams. Only the "old guard" of planned economy advocates and jealous academicians who had missed the boat were able to shut their eyes to the moral and economic justification of this liberating break through in international development policy spearheaded by the Bretton Woods institutions then steered by some exceptionally courageous economists.

Reaction to Saps

As with any revolution, defeat is awaiting the pioneers at the hands of political power greed, reactionary tactics by the formerly privileged and academic envy. The principal device serving the reactionary forces as a lever of influence on the mood of the "development community" has been the identification and dramatisation of new pockets or strata of (principally urban) poverty allegedly created by structural adjustment measures, while shunning the much broader-based rise in economic activity, real incomes and sense of fair reward in the overall society, especially the rural population. That the hardship experienced by urban poor, formerly privileged under consumer price control and import subsidies to the debit of depressed farm prices or maintained by grossly over-expanded public payrolls, was only laying open the camouflaged erosion of the economy and near-bankruptcy of governments and public enterprises was conveniently downplayed.

These reactionary howls were to be expected. Not that they met the entirely innocent. There had been naively sweeping, overly assuming demands by some structural adjustment missions. But an intellectually vigorous and dynamic "development community" would have coped with the ensuing opposition, strengthened the analytical and monitoring capacities and the political will to endure also rocky roads and bitter medicines on the way to a healthier base. Instead, institutional rivalry, political opportunism and emotive populism were thriving. In a way, the "development community" behaved as if it did not want its patient to become able to stand on his own feet and eventually steal its *raison d'etre.*

Worst, the Bretton Woods institutions themselves, partly under the pressure of the emotive opposition described above fell to the temptation to rescue their lending volume, which was threatened by the frugality dictated to third World public budgets under structural adjustment recipes, through hardship-easing loans. They thereby corrupted their creation in using it to reinforce their indispensability. As a consequence it soon turned out that some of the most obedient loan takers under structural adjustment terms experienced sharply rising indebtedness, exploited as a disqualifying symptom by the anti-structural adjustment camp.

Whatever the opinions on structural adjustment policies, the commitment to the principles of "good governance" has come to stay, at least on paper, as an almost standard conditionally for official development aid from OECD donor countries. The realisation, matured in the implementation of structural adjustment programmes, that not the quantity of aid, but the quality of Third World governments determines the positive or negative course of development, may be regarded as the most valuable fruit of the decades-old policy debate in the 'development community". And the use of aid as a pressure or bribing factor towards "good governance" as foreign aid's least disputable purpose.

Out of the Limelight

Nothing, however, must be taken for granted. Achievement breeds its challenge! Structural adjustment, though in essence hardly disputable has been pushed out of the limelight and replaced by the oldest actor in the company: eradication of poverty, twinned with an equally perpetual endeavour at the macro-level: debt-forgiveness. This falling back to square one in donors' approach to the problems of the south, i.e., the call to alleviate poverty and priorities direct efforts to this end above all other developmental efforts—does it indicate a sell-out of constructive ideas in the "development community"? Has any noteworthy progress been achieved in the past by this approach?

By telling a frugally toiling but independent subsistence farmer that internationally his condition is classed as "poverty", deserving compassion and support by the world community and cancellation of his debts, one can hardly expect a sustainable improvement in his output, satisfaction, or self-respect and even less, when he realises that the help principally provides jobs, fringe benefits and self-importance to a gamut of intermediaries, at home and abroad.

What do those poverty advocates (the "Lords of poverty") really know about the resources, life management, value systems and ambitions of those they generalise by the billions? The great variance in the conception of life situations, from different external viewpoints.

What the aid system can do for these rural populations classed as "poor"/"underprivileged"/"exploited", is press for justice, i.e., "good governance". The achievements of structural adjustment policy through e.g., abolishing official price and exchange rate distortions, import subsidies and exploitative state agencies, has brought massive income improvement for peasant populations, i.e., the majority of LDC inhabitants, in dimensions unreachable by whatsoever direct "attack" on rural "poverty". What people want is not being benevolently treated as poor, but being justly rewarded for their work, i.e., by access to the unmanipulated market value of their output. Slackening on structural adjustment/"good governance" conditionally under the present" 10-year itch" for paradigm change means forgoing much of the potential opportunities for undoing injustice and exploitation of the masses. It should be clear where priority focus should be placed in ODA policy.

Small is not Beautiful

The direct attack on "poverty", orchestrated by the Bretton Woods institutions under their freshly launched Poverty Reduction Strategy Paper (PRSP) campaign, is being rightly regarded as primarily an NGO domain, since most activities are expected to be carried out at local community level. This would require careful screening and coordinating of NGO activities and their integration via gradual expansion of their experience. But "small" is not "beautiful" for the development financing institutions. Disbursement needs are pressing, calling for the new paradigm to quickly provide channels for another wave of loans to the "IDA countries". Their problem of heavy indebtedness, which would principally exclude most of them from any new loan consideration, shall be solved with one stroke (which only the well-cushioned development bureaucracy can afford); debt relief against presentation of country PRSPs by the respective governments. NGOs are expected to play in the system especially the knowledge gap about the "poor" people's real wants and needs NGOs will naturally be tempted by such expansionary boost to their involvement (referred to sarcastically as their philanthropic empire" by an African conference participant), but this will not be conducive to quality and accountability of their performance, which ideally should be based on private sponsorship in combination with strong target-group provided self-help components.

Patience and Self-Restraint

Local knowledge and initiatives cannot be obtained under time pressure. "The grass does not grow faster by being pulled". When will the "development community" learn patience and self-restraint in the approach to LDC's capacity for constructive absorption of aid programmes accompanied by a genuine sense of ownership?

After all these deliberations, how shall development policy be shaped in order to better correspond with reality, without sinking deeper into hypocrisy and frustration?

To come back to the opening question: what was wrong with "structural adjustment"? Nothing was wrong with its intent. In fact this was very right and long overdue. Its implementation, however, lacked patience, perseverance and solid support from the development community, apart from its being corrupted as a vehicle for expansionary lending policy. If aid is meant to not be an end in itself, then structural adjustment policy needs constant reinforcement, underpinned by strict lending discipline. There should be an end to irresponsible lending and easy escape from its consequences by wholesome periodic debt relief burdened on the international tax-paying community. No ODA, either loans or grants, should be made available to governments who are not in active process of implementing "good governance" principles. A monitoring unit, reporting to the donor community on government performance in regard to its" good government"? Structural adjustment commitment, should be maintained in each and receiving country by "donor consortia" comprising all locally represented bilateral and multilateral development organisations currently extending technical, financial or material assistance to the country.

In order to accommodate the poverty focus without diluting the necessary structural adjustment orientation of ODA, a division of activity-focus between the latter and the NGO sector would seem to be advantageous.

- ODA, limited to the countries abiding to structural adjustment/"good governance" conditionally, with focus concentration on sustainable physical, social and economic infrastructure principally at national and regional level, public management training, higher education and research, consultant and senior adviser services.
- the NGO sector, principally funded by private sponsorship, united to structural adjustment conditionally (but preferably grafted on local self-help initiative), with focus-concentration on the "third

World "poor", i.e., mostly at rural community and low-income township level, for amelioration of living conditions and local resource utilisation.

- strengthening of linkages between the NGO sector and the UN Technical Agencies to mutual benefit: NGOs in need of professional information, evaluation and advice or forum for discussion to find an actively supportive window at the agencies: the latter to maintain and develop field contact for research and policy generation, not least as a substitute for their declining project work (giving way to greater concentration on their global functions i.e., serving as information, policy initiation, and coordination/ negotiation center on topics of global concern, such as e.g. human rights, global monetary and trade systems, tropical forest and global marine resources, global and regional health threats, international standards.)

In conclusion, it may be called to mind that aid and its institutions have no claim for permanence. They are justified only as temporary functions in a phasing-out process of self-help support. Any claim for unlimited continuity would breed lasting infantilisation.

Chapter—13

Taking Poverty to Heart

Non-Communlicable Diseases and the Poor

Non-Communicable Diseases (NCDs) are the leading cause of death worldwide. Their emergence as the predominant health problem in wealthy countries accompanied economic development. As a result, NCDs are often referred to as 'diseases of affluence'. But is this a misleading term? It suggests that these are not major problems for the world's poor, which is quite simply wrong, as this article illustrates. Is it time to rethink policy on NCDs?

NCDs include cardiovascular disease (CVD), such as stroke and heart attack, diabetes, chronic lung disease, cancer, diseases of bones and joint, and mental illness. The single biggest killer is coronary heart disease, followed by other CVDs, cancer and chronic lung disease. Diabetes is a major contributor to deaths from CVD, but also causes its own unique complications. Common risk factors for these conditions include smoking, physical activity, obesity and diets high in saturated fat and sodium and low in fruit and vegetables.

By 2020, NCDs will be the biggest cause of death in all regions apart from sub-Saharan Africa. It is predicted that in 2010, the number of people with diabetes worldwide will be double the level in 1995 and that the biggest increase (both proportionately and in absolute number) will be in poorer regions. CVD occurs at an earlier age in developing countries, increasing the potential adverse economic and social consequences.

NCDs are already major health problems for adults in the poorest countries of the world. Demographic data show that age-specific death rates from NCDs in Tanzania are higher than in wealthier countries. Mortality rates for some NCDs, such as stroke, are particularly high. However, while NCDs account for 80 per cent of adult deaths in developed regions, the figure is less than 30 per cent in Tanzania, reflecting the continuing burden of infectious disease. Countries like Tanzania suffer the 'worst of both worlds'. Even within a country, 'diseases of affluence' is a misleading term. A more accurate label is 'diseases of urbanisation'. Several studies from developing countries show increased levels of high blood pressure and other NCD risk factors in urban compared to rural populations. Even within urban areas, the more affluent do not always suffer the greatest burden.

The rise of NCDs in developing countries is inextricably linked to economic and cultural globalisation. This is exemplified by the activities of multinational tobacco companies. Tobacco-related deaths will exceed the toll due to HIV and become the single largest preventable cause of death by 2020. Curbing the effects of globalisation on the prevention and treatment of NCDs will also require regulation of food and agriculture multinationals and the pharmaceutical and healthcare industries.

Much of the projected rise in NCDs is preventable, particularly that due to smoking, poor diet, physical inactivity and obesity. Early action in some populations could prevent the emergence of these risk factors altogether; in others, the challenge is to reduce established levels. Although it is unclear whether all major risk factors are equally important in every region, the strength and consistency of data on the core risk factors in several ethnic groups justify preventative action now.

Lessons from risk factor intervention studies in rich and middle income countries suggest that success requires:

- Broad intersectoral action
- Community participation
- Appropriate legislation
- Involvement of appropriate NGOs
- Health services changes to manage those at high risk and promote public education.

Even apparently minor changes, such as a small fall in average population blood pressure, can have substantial benefits. However, some preventative programmes have produced disappointing results and almost all have failed to halt the ubiquitous increase in obesity. This highlights the difficulty of promoting healthy behaviour by individuals who are surrounded by barriers to change and inducements to lead an unhealthy lifestyle.

Health systems in developing countries face both a growing need for prevention programmes and increasing numbers of individuals requiring treatment. The complications of high blood pressure and diabetes can be reduced by the delivery of effective healthcare. Crucially this entails:

- Partnership between patients and health professionals with the knowledge, ability and resources to take appropriate measures over many years
- Cheap and effective drugs and the implementation of simple treatment protocols, as promoted by WHO and the CVD initiative of the Global Forum for Health Research.

An appropriate policy and strategic framework is essential for such initiatives to be effective on a large scale. Even in the poorest countries people are already seeking healthcare for NCDs in both the public and private sectors, particularly in urban areas. Whatever the balance of priorities between different conditions, existing resources should be used as effectively as possible. Rapid evaluation methods can provide policy-makers with information on the current levels and quality of care and identify the main opportunities for improving health services.

The proper planning and co-ordination of NCD prevention and treatment, whether globally or nationally, requires up-to-date data on risk factor and disease levels—currently missing for much of the world. To address this lack, the WHO Non-Communicable Disease and Mental Health Surveillance section is promoting a standardised approach to enable comparisons across regions and over time, preparing the first ever 'world risk status' report for the major NCDs. This will provide a truly global perspective on the size and nature of the problem.

As this article has shown, NCDs are major health problems even in the world's poorest countries, including those regions where infectious diseases continue to take a huge toll. The NCD burden will grow substantially in low land middle-income countries over the next 10 to 20 years. NCDs will increasingly demand attention and require the right balance between competing priorities for prevention, cure and care. In meeting this challenge, national policy-makers will need to follow the lead of WHO and develop a strategic framework that plans for surveillance, prevention and appropriate health sector reforms.

Chapter—14

Richer or Poorer?

Achievements and Challenges of Ethical Trade

Ethical trade as an approach to supply chain management has mushroomed in recent years. Northern companies are becoming increasingly concerned with the 'ethics' of their operations and the risks to reputation and productivity posed by bad employment practices in global supply chains. But can voluntary private sector codes really improve employment conditions in supply chains?

Ethical trade is one dimension of corporate social responsibility, bringing social issues into the mainstream of commercial supply chain management through the use of codes of conduct. It is sometimes confused with fair-trade which addresses terms of trading for smaller producers, and fosters greater responsibility in supply chain relations.

Ethical trade, on the other hand, focuses on workplace issues, requiring that suppliers in particular meet minimum employment, worker welfare and aspects of human rights standards.

Similar management systems are well established for product safety and environmental issues. Here, we focus on the social dimensions of ethical trade and its codes of conduct yet the separation of social and environmental standards is increasingly artificial in global sourcing agreements. A plethora of codes are on offer. The most numerous are in-houses codes such as Nike's 233 company codes were counted in 1999 and the figure is rising.

Suppliers have to comply with and pay for a multitude of similar but different codes. Harmonising codes or establishing equivalence is on the agènda but has not yet halted the problem of 'code overload'.

At a broader level, industry-specific codes have also been developed. The US Apparel Industry Partnership/Fair Labour Agreement adopted by a number of leading US merchandising companies is a good example. Industry standards are not new, as ISO and EMAS environmental management systems show. Building on ISO principles, Social Accountability International (formerly CEPAA) has developed SA8000. This is an independent social standard that can be used as an auditable code throughout the private sector.

Ethical trade is partly a response to consumer and campaigning group pressure in globalised economy. Alliances of companies, NGOs, trade. Developing codes of conduct through a multi stakeholder approach is a striking aspect of ethical trade, bringing together companies, NGOs, trade unions and some government departments. An example of this collaborative approach is the Ethical Trading Initiative (ETI) in the UK. The ETI's baseline code of conduct that corporate members from various industries must comply with as a minimum standard is more than just a code. ETI aims to provide a learning environment and sponsors pilot projects in developing countries to test different methods of monitoring and verification.

Codes of conduct need to be assessed in terms of content, implantation and impact. A number of professional auditing companies have moved into this area, some accredited to audit specific codes such as FLA or SA8000. Suppliers audited against a specific code undergo an inspection, and where non-compliance is found, have to take remedial action or risk failing the audit.

Social auditing is a complex process, however, and it can be difficult to sport work place abuse, such as sexual harassment or forced overtime, Workers have little confidence in a process that appears to be linked with management, and fear that reporting issues could risk their jobs. Advocates of the multi stakeholder approach argue that effective monitoring and verification of codes must involve local NGOs and trade unions in which workers have trust. Participatory social auditing also a means of raising awareness and of facilitating behavioral change, can help reveal serious management problems. But in many developing countries local organisations lack the capacity to participate: developing sustainable local systems of monitoring and verification remain an important challenge.

Do the advantages of multi-stakeholder approaches outweigh immediate constraints? Ethical trade is a largely northern driven process, reflecting Wastern ethical thinking and priorities, Southern based initiatives, however, are expanding, raising the possibility of local ownership of codes. Collaboration poses challenges. Stronger relationships and better understanding are essential between southern and northern workers, producers, trade unions, and NGOs for codes to work globally.

But there is still scepticism as to the extent of the benefits that ethical trade might bring. Will increasing southern capacity to participate, as the ETI has done in its pilot project, help? Will building trust, confidence and dialogue achieve the objectives of ethical trade, north and south? Child labour is often more complex, however, than codes make it appear. Codes need to address the conditions of all workers within the supply chain, including the least visible: partnerships must include all groups to address these limitations.

The role of government is hotly contested. Can a system whose credibility depends on under-resourced civil society actors, often excluding democratically elected representatives, maintain genuine credibility? If the boundaries between private sector and public sector roles are not defined, the list of private sector responsibilities will become unmanageable. Private sector initiatives are not a substitute for more comprehensive national or international development policies.

What are the consequences of codes? Do they encourage downsizing or reinforce from large suppliers where compliance is more easily monitored? There is a risk that the gains of some will be at the expense of others.

Ethical trade has successfully begun forging partnerships to find solutions. While it might be wrong to assume that ethical trade can change the world, handled wisely, it could make a world of difference for some. Yet it is not a panacea for development. Issues that remain unchallenged by ethical trade include:

- The exclusion of companies producing for domestic markets—often bigger employers.
- Underlying causes of poverty and social marginalisation.

Chapter—15
Pro-Poor Tourism

Opportunities for Sustainable Local Development

Tourism is the world's largest industry, with over 10 per cent of GDP globally directly related to tourism activities. Rising standards of living in the countries of the North, declining long-haul travel costs, increasing holiday entitlements, changing demographics and strong consumer demand for exotic international travel have resulted in significant tourism growth to developing countries. Tourism is the principal export for one-third of developing countries. Tourism brings relatively powerful consumers to Southern countries, potentially an important market for local entrepreneurs and an engine for local sustainable economic development. There is no reliable data on domestic tourism but it is growing rapidly in South America and in China and South East Asia; it represents a very significant economic opportunity for many local communities.

Tourism and Aid

Multilateral and bilateral aid agencies are wary of involving themselves in the tourism sector. In 1969 the World Bank created a Tourism Projects Department recognising that in the Mediterranean and Adriatic countries, and in Mexico, tourism had been a significant generator of foreign exchange and of direct and indirect employment, internationally in the late nineteen sixties, there was considerable concern about high rates of unemployment and the ability of developing countries to service debt. Tourism sector studies were completed in some 31 countries and tourism staff regularly participated in World Bank macro-economic missions—their reports focussed on the potential for growth in tax revenues, foreign exchange earnings and direct and indirect employment effects. The primary emphasis was on national economic impact. By 1978 when the World Bank closed its Tourism Projects Department the Bank had provided loans and credits for 18 projects in 14 countries and it was the major source of funds and technical assistance for tourism development. The bank withdrew from tourism development for a range of reasons amongst which were anxieties about the role of the bank in funding projects to develop luxury hotels designed to attract wealthy travellers from the developed countries. This strategy was seen inconsistent with new policy objectives which prioritised the bottom 40 per cent, the Bank's priorities were shifting towards the poor, a group, which was gaining relatively little from tourism development. There was a growing literature that focussed on the negative economic, social and cultural impacts of unmanaged tourism on local communities. The fuel crises of the nineteen seventies also undermined some of the forecasts that had been made for the strength of the market and the Bank withdrew from the sector in parallel with most other multilateral and bilateral agencies.

The international agencies followed a macro-economic tourism agenda in the nineteen seventies and eighties focusing on tax and foreign exchange revenues at the national level, major hotel and resort development, international promotion and national and regional master planning all attracted funding. In the nineties the adoption of the new poverty elimination target of halving the number of people living on less than 1 US $ per day by 2015 refocused development assistance on pro-poor growth. Multilateral and bilateral aid agency agendas are shifting towards microeconomic growth strategies, which benefit local communities and in particular those below the poverty threshold. With poverty elimination now at the heart of decision aid, the potential for using tourism to generate pro-poor economic growth is being reassessed.

Since the mid-1980s, interest in 'green' tourism, eco-tourism and community tourism has grown rapidly among tour operators, policy makers, advocates and researchers. All of these focus on the need to ensure that tourism does not erode the environmental and cultural base on which it depends. The emphasis has been on minimising social, cultural and environmental impacts; rather than on positively affecting the livelihoods of the poor.

The Potential of Pro-Poor Tourism

There are a number of reasons to look again at tourism and to assess its potential to generate pro-poor growth. Eighty per cent of the world's poor live in just 12 countries and tourism is significant or growing in all but one of them. Tourism is a very large sector, it is growing rapidly, and there is some evidence that it is relatively labour intensive. The consumer travels to the destination, creating additional— local—opportunities for the sale of additional goods and services—ranging from local pottery to a guided walk. Tourism can be used to diversify local economics; it can often be developed in remote and marginal areas with few other diversifications or export opportunities. These areas often attract tourists because of their high landscape, cultural and wildlife values. These natural resources and the local culture are amongst the few assets of the poor.

Pro-poor tourism generates net benefits for the poor. It can be defined as forms of tourism where the benefits to the poor are greater than costs which tourism brings them. Economic costs and benefits are clearly important but social environmental and cultural costs and benefits are clearly important, but social benefits also need to be taken into account. Pro-poor tourism aims to expand opportunities for those living on less than 1 US$ per day. Whilst it will also need to be sustainable preserving local culture, minimizing environmental impacts, it will be driven by the poverty agenda. Community-based tourism seeks to promote initiatives by local communities or individuals within them; much has been learnt from these projects. Maximizing the poverty elimination effect requires that the emphasis is placed on involving those people who are living on less than 1 US $ per day and creating economic opportunities for them. Not all community tourism is pro-poor in this sense.

Effects on the Livelihoods of the Poor

Assessing the livelihood impacts of tourism is not simply a matter of counting jobs or wage income. Participatory poverty assessments demonstrate great variety in the priorities of the poor and factors affecting livelihood security and sustainability. Tourism can affect many of these, positively and negatively, often indirectly. It is important to assess these impacts and their distribution.

Tourism can generate four different types of local cash income generally involving different categories of people:

- wages from formal employment;
- earnings from selling goods, services, or casual labour (e.g., food, crafts, building materials, guide services);
- and profits arising from locally owned enterprises
- Income: this may include profits from a community run enterprise, dividends from a private sector partnership and land rental paid by an investor.

Waged employment can be sufficient to lift a household from insecure to secure. But it may only be available to a minority, and not to the poor. Casual earnings per person may be very small, but much more widely spread and may be enough, for instance, to cover school fees for one or more children. Work as a tourist guide although casual, is often of high status and relatively well paid. There are relatively few examples of successful and sustainable collective income from tourism.

Negative economic impacts include inflation, dominance by outsiders in land markets and in-migration, which erodes economic opportunities for the local poor. Impacts differ between men and women. Women can be the first to suffer from loss of natural resources (e.g., access to fuel wood) and cultural/sexual exploitation, but may benefit most from physical infrastructure improvements (e.g. piped water or a grinding mill) where this is a by-product of tourism.

Positive Development Impacts of Tourism

On the positive side, tourism can generate funds for investment in health, education and other assets, provide infrastructure, stimulate development of social capital, strengthen sustainable management of natural resources, and create a demand for improved assets (especially education). On the negative side, tourism can reduce local access to natural resources draw heavily upon local infrastructure, and disrupt social networks.

Tourism affects the livelihoods of the poor by changing their access to assets. In several cases, tourism's impact on people's access to natural resources or physical infrastructure has been identified as the most important benefit or concern.

Cultural Impacts of Tourism can be Positive or Negative

Local residents often highlight the way tourism affects other livelihood goals—whether positively or negatively—such as cultural pride, a sense of control, good health, and reduced vulnerability. Socio-cultural intrusion by tourists is often cited as a negative impact. Certainly sexual exploitation particularly affects the poorest women, girls and young men. The poor themselves may view other types of cultural change as positive. Tourism can also increase the value attributed to minority cultures by national policy-makers. Overall, the cultural impacts of tourism are hard to disentangle from wider processes of development.

The overall balance of positive and negative livelihood impacts will vary enormously between situations, among people and over time, and particularly in the extent to which local priorities are able to influence the planning process. The application of a 'sustainable' livelihood framework is essential to developing pro-poor approaches. The distribution of livelihood impacts has to be considered. The poor are far from being a homogeneous group. The positive and negative impacts of tourism will inevitably be distributed unevenly among poor groups, reflecting different patterns of assets, activities, opportunities and choices. The most substantial benefits, particularly jobs, may be concentrated among few. Net benefits are likely to be smallest, or negative, for the poorest.

Policies to Enhance Pro-Poor Tourism

Despite innumerable case studies of tourism development there is relatively little assessment of practical experience in strategies to make tourism more pro-poor. Nevertheless, lessons can be drawn from a wealth of small initiatives (many from 'community tourism' or 'conservation and development' programmes), supplemented by expanding knowledge on 'pro-poor growth strategies', several policy implications clearly emerge.

1. *Put Poverty Issues on the Tourism Agenda*

A first step is to recognise that enhancing the poverty impacts of tourism is different from commercial, environmental or ethical concerns. PPT can be incorporated as an additional objective, but this requires pro-active and strategic intervention. There may well be trade-offs to make—for example between attracting all-inclusive operators and maximising informal sector opportunities, or between faster growth through outside investment, and slower growth building on the local capacity. These trade-offs need to be addressed.

2. *Enhance Economic Opportunities and a Wide Range of Impacts*

Two approaches need to be combined:

- Expand poor people's economic participation by addressing the barriers they face, and maximising a wide range of employment, self-employment and informal sector opportunities;
- Incorporate wider concerns of the poor into decision-making. Reducing competition for natural resources, minimising trade-offs with other livelihood activities, using tourism to create physical infrastructure that benefits the poor and addressing cultural disruption will often be particularly important.

3. *A Multi-Level Approach*

Pro-poor interventions can and should be taken at three different levels:

- this is where pro-active practical partnerships can be developed between operators, residents, NGOs and local authorities, to maximise benefits;
- national policy level-policy reform may be needed on a range of tourism issues (planing, licensing, training)

and non-tourism issues (land tenure, business incentives, infrastructure, land-use planning);

- International level—to encourage responsible consumer and business behaviour, and to enhance commercial codes of conduct.

4. *Work Through Partnerships, Including Business and Tourists*

National and local governments, private enterprises, industry associations, NGOs, community organisations, consumers, and donors all have a role to play. It is particularly important to engage business, and to ensure that initiatives are commercially realistic and integrated into main stream operations. Private operators will not be able to devote substantial time and resources to developing pro-poor actions. NGOs and donors can help in reducing the transaction costs of changing commercial practice—for example, facilitating the training, organisation, and communication that would enable businesses to use more local suppliers. Changing the attitudes of tourists (at both international and national levels) is also essential if pro-poor tourism is to be commercially viable and sustainable.

5. *Incorporate Pro-Poor Tourism Approaches into Mainstream Tourism*

Pro-poor tourism should not just be pursued in niche markets (such as eco-tourism or community tourism). It is even more important that mass tourism is developed in ways that benefit the poor. It is also important to assess which tourism segments are particularly relevant to the poor. Domestic tourists are likely to be important customers.

6. *Reform Decision-Making Systems*

It is impossible to prescribe exactly how each tourism enterprise should develop in ways that best fit with livelihoods. The most important principle is to enhance the participation of the poor. Three different ways of doing this can be identified:

- Strengthen rights at local level (e.g., tenure over tourism assets), so that local people have market power and make their own decisions over developments.

- Develop more participatory planning.
- Use planning gain and other incentives to encourage private investors to enhance local benefits. These approaches require implementation capacity among governmental and non-governmental institutions within the destination, and require a supportive national policy framework.

It is time to reconsider the role of tourism in contributing to prò-poor development. Tourism should be judged against other possible strategies and where it offers the best opportunities for pro-poor growth, or where it can make a useful contribution by increasing the diversity of opportunities for the poor, tourism it should be considered. However, careful and effective local management will be essential if it is to contribute to meeting poverty targets and if tourism dependency is to be avoided.

Chapter—16
Venture Capital for Small and Medium Business

A Proposal for South-South Cooperation

Although great strides have been made in the last decade to help finance business start-ups for micro-enterprises in low-income countries (LICs), using models such as the Grameen Bank in Bangladesh and others, no similar initiative has been taken to help small and medium enterprises (SMEs) in these countries.

Development banks or other development finance institutions (DFIs) in developing countries are not really meant nor organized to serve the particular needs of their countries' SMEs. They are not only unable to draw on a local capital market to finance their operations, but they also lack the range of advisory services required by SMEs to submit bankable loan applications and are themselves ill-equipped to evaluate such applications. Consequently, they concentrate on a few large projects—preferably of the infrastructure type—for which they rely on the technical expertise of the foreign donors financing them or specially hired consultants.

In the absence of a realistic access to DFIs, SMEs have been constrained to seek their loans for new business ventures from commercial banks. The fact that since 1978 the World Bank has been challenging a large portion of its credit lines intended for SMEs through commercial banks rather than through DFIs, reflects the importance which donors attach to the role of LIC commercial banks as the principal intermediaries for SME lending.

Reasons for Failure of Traditional Banking Systems

However, there are several important reasons why commercial banks are ill-suited to perform this task. First and foremost, the banking systems of these countries were conceived during a period when most investment capital was provided by the government, usually drawing on foreign aid. Thus, even in those LICs which had not entirely succumbed to the socialist ideology in the sense of eliminating all private enterprise, commercial banks continue to limit their credit activity largely to self-liquidating, low-risk credits seldom exceeding 12 months' duration, preferably conventional trade credits. Secondly, even in the exceptional cases where commercial banks in these countries entertain applications for medium-term credits to finance the launching of a small manufacturing project, they will normally demand ironclad collateral in the forms of liens on real-estate and/or personal guarantees by friends and relatives with similar backing, unless the applicant is a well-known customer of the bank.

Thirdly, with their overriding concern for profitability, most LIC commercial banks tend to like upon business start-up loans to SMEs as being too risky and/or administratively too costly to handle in relation to the loan amounts involved. For these reasons, commercial banks in these countries are unlikely to establish in-house facilities to meet the specific needs of SMEs, such as helping them in project preparation and market analysis. Last but not least, factors such as the project's development orientation" (e.g. its important substitution and export potential, its ability to increase productivity and its employment generation features) do not enter into the calculations of commercial banks which will orient their actions towards "bottom line" results and risk minimization. Under the circumstances, most commercial banks are not inclined to become directly involved in project supervision, as long as their customers' repayment records are satisfactory.

Credit for SMEs

Whereas new approaches have been developed over the last decade by various development assistance agencies to help upgrade commercial banks' staff capability, especially in advising

SME borrowers in such maters as project formulation and market analysis as well as improving and market analysis as well as improving their loan repayment capacity, only recently has an effort been made to find ways and means of making investment capital available to SME entrepreneurs for launching new businesses. In some LICs, lines of credit have been established by multilateral or bilateral banks from which loan capital can be sought for such projects, but only seldom has genuine risk (i.e., equity) capital been made available and when some only through the donors' own agencies. The interest rate charged by the local banks for administering loans from these credit lines in local currency are generally at a par with existing commercial rates, which tend to be prohibitive for a new venture of the type being promoted. These high rates are due to several factors, including (a) the local rates of inflation and the consequent devaluation risks, (b) the high risk factor of the new enterprises with little or no collateral and credit standing, and (c) the lack of experience of bank staff in the evaluation of loan requests submitted to them for unfamiliar projects. Significantly, most international DFIs are loath to lower interest rates to be applied on loans financed by their credit lines, lest they be accused of unfair competition on the local financial markets.

Incentives Ineffective in Attracting Foreign Investors

Although many international conferences, investment promotion meetings and other fora have been staged by UN bodies and donor groups to generate private investor interest in the LICs, these efforts have proved largely ineffectual. While much has been done by LIC governments in recent years to create a more attractive "enabling environment" for private investment, these incentives have been necessary but not sufficient to convince developed-country enterprises or investors to assume the necessary risks, with the exception of selected sectors such as mineral extraction, tourism and a narrow range of exportable consumer goods, such as out-of-season fruits and vegetables, and tropical products such as cocoa and certain spices. Even public support for project preparation has ultimately failed to provide preparation has ultimately failed to provide private business in industrial countries the incentives needed to take an active role in a broadly-based economic development of LICs.

The bottomline for potential investors in LICs is constituted by the profits which their investment will yield within a reasonable period of time, under conditions which offer a reasonable amount of political and legal stability. So far, these basic conditions have not been met on the whole. In the new global economy with its almost total reliance on free market principles and the ability to choose investment sites freely, the choice is not likely to fall on the LICs, but rather on a small number of more advanced developing countries, apart from the industrial countries themselves.

South-to-South Technological/Commercial Cooperation

While the inherent disadvantages faced by LICs in competing for foreign investment capital are too great to be overcome by a magic panacea, any attempt at a solution must include measures designed to mobilize the entrepreneurial abilities and dynamism available in existing and potential SMEs engaged in production of a variety of goods destined for the broad consumer market at home and abroad. In most LICs such existing or potential SMEs need to access affordable foreign technologies, i.e., the machinery and the technological know-how required to install and make the machinery function. One of the prime sources of such technologies for LICs can be found in enterprises in South/Southeast Asia and China, countries that have only recently graduated from the LIC status (or have not yet done so but have nevertheless managed to create a modern industrial sector within their overall state of underdevelopment and poverty). The concretization of transfers of technology from these countries to the LICs is especially affected by the financing problems described above, because in the normal case neither one of the potential partners can afford the necessary venture, even though they can and will invest their know-how, time and very often land, buildings and infrastructure. This problem is much less acute in the case of the more expensive, and hence often unaffordable "Northern" technologies, where the technology provider finds it easier to mobilize start-up capital from its own resources or by borrowing from his commercial bank against his firms' overall credit line.

The underlying economic rationale in favour of such South-to-South, company-to-company transfers of production technology argues that Asian firms can help launch industrial start-ups in these countries far more cheaply and quickly than the more sophisticated companies from the North. By offering labour-intensive rather than capital-intensive production machinery accompanied by vitally needed on-the-job training, back-up managerial and maintenance follow-up at a fraction of the cost of Northern firms, Asian companies' cooperation can spell the difference between a successful business start-up and a failed one. Furthermore Asian-sourced machinery can be operated at production scales corresponding to the reduced market requirements and limited purchasing power of most LIC markets.

In view of the above described financing problems faced by South-to-South deals, it is proposed that a Venture Capital Fund by established specializing in the provision of equity capital for joint ventures (JVs) among SMEs in various LICs. In many cases the existence of such a Fund—which might be called the Venture Capital Fund or simply (VENCAP) – will spell the difference between business proposals that are still-born for want of the required initial financing, and profitable ventures which are launched thanks to the missing—if minority—equity contribution from the Fund.

Characteristics of the Fund

The proposed VENCAP would be expected to be an active participant in the project in which it will invest, sharing its financial and strategic vision with the invested firm. To this end, it must have access to experienced project evaluation specialists with intimate knowledge of conditions in low-income countries in general, and the project and its promoters in particular. As might be expected, the Fund would concentrate its resources in early-state financing, rather than in plant expansion or replacement, inasmuch as the projects likely to be the most profitable are the new ones, which will normally start from empty factory buildings and offices, where only a minimum amount of production equipment, if any, is normally usable for the operation of the new JV.

The Fund would limit its participation to joint ventures in which firms of at least two developing countries hold equity stakes, although firm from developed countries might also participate. The FUND would limit its participation to production JVs whose total initial capital would not exceed a given sum to be determined. Its own participation would in turn also be limited by a relative ceiling per venture i.e., a maximum percentage of the total capital. This combination would implicitly set an absolute ceiling to the Fund's participation in any given JV.

Success and Selection Criteria

The number of proposed projects must be sufficient to allow the Fund to pick and choose the best. A good ratio of applications to acceptances might be in the range of 10:1 Whereas commercial viability will constitute the first and foremost selection criterion, every effort would be made to select projects which have a strong development character, are environmentally friendly and/or involve production technologies which are deemed to be vital and critical to the recipient country's current socio-economic needs. Thus, preference would be given to sectors such as (a) food processing, (b) water purification, (c) renewable energy, (d) agricultural development, and (e) light engineering. In all cases, the emphasis would be on cost-effective, labour-intensive production technologies.

The Fund's avility to divest itself of its participation at a profit will be the ultimate test of the Fund's success. Ideally, the Fund should be able to do this within a maximum of one or two years, so as to enable it to effectively cycle its resources to other equally meritorious projects.

Proposals for VENCAP's Organisational Structure

Besides being run by an experienced Fund manager, VENCAP would be assisted in its investment decisions by National Advisory Committees (NACs), which would be established in all participating LICs and would be composed of prominent business persons, professional men and women and financiers. These NACs would be chaired by an experienced consultant/consulting firm selected by the Fund. No member of the NAC having business or family links with the person or firm applying for equity financing would participate in the evaluation procedure. VENCAP would be represented on the Boards of

Directors of the firms in which it has acquired minority stakes through one or several members of the relevant NAC. The Fund itself would be run by a Board of Directors in which all of the major investors would be represented (and possibly some NGOs, PVOs).

Follow-up

It is hoped that this article will provoke sufficient interest to justify the convening of an international meeting of aid agency officials and experts to study the ideas set forth above, so as to facilitate VENCAP's formal launching as an operative force. The need is there, the customers are there, the goodwill is there, only the financing and the organization are lacking!

Chapter—17

Law and Social Justice

Law reform in the service of democracy must find ways of protecting the vulnerable. Legal reform and "good governance" have vaulted to the top of the development agenda. International financial institutions and influential donors continually stress the importance of the rule of law, a healthy regulatory environment and strong and consistent enforcement of rights to successful economic development. In the new world order, the state's role is to facilitate private activity rather than guarantee the welfare of its citizens.

But there is growing concern that market reforms and globalization are connected to greater social stratification and economic inequality. What is often overlooked is that legal reform may enhance rather than alleviate this stratification and inequality.

It is important to see legal reform as a key part of a broader set of policy, legislative and institutional reforms which are designed to create not simply rule—and norm-based societies but particular types of market economies. There are no "free" markets; functioning markets depend upon a legal infrastructure and a commitment to the rule of law. The growing interest in legal reform indicates nothing if not the widespread recognition of this fact.

Tradeoffs between Efficiency and Equity

Respecting the rule of law and protecting rights however does not mean that there is any one best set of laws, even in a market economy. Yet legal reform projects in developing and transitional countries have become inseparably associated with the idea of single, optimal path or model. Current projects emphasize strong protection for property rights, the consistent enforcement of contracts and, increasingly, financial sector regulation as the foundation of an investor-friendly legal infrastructure. At the same time, states in transition to markets have been discouraged from adopting or retaining "excessive" regulations, including protective labour market policies that might impede growth and efficiency.

Market-oriented legal reforms can affect the fortunes of different groups in at least three different ways. The first is through the types of reforms that are implemented. Because legal reforms allocate rights and entitlements, because legal reforms allocate rights and entitlements, different rule structures may well benefit different groups in different ways. In some instances, there may be tradeoffs between efficiency and equity. Strong property rights will protect owners and entrepreneurs but may contribute to the disadvantage of renters and works; environmental and consumer protection laws protect the public at large but impose costs on businesses.

Second, people can be affected by the absence of particular laws. Labour standards and laws authorizing collective bargaining, for example, have been crucial in industrialized societies. If they are weak or missing as they are in many developing countries, or if they are indefinitely postponed because priority is given to implementing laws and regulations which facilitate economic transactions, vast numbers of people can find themselves worse off than they need be in the market for labour. Particular groups may also be harmed. Women with caregiving obligations are likely to be systematically disadvantaged and shut out of better work opportunities without market regulations which ensure that part of these costs are borne by others. This is especially likely where social programmes and subsidies are reduced or eliminated at the same time, as has occurred in many parts of the world.

Open Debate

Finally, where legal reforms follow a "standard form" or are designed by experts from afar, a common experience in transitional states, the risk is that local history and priorities will be ignored or displaced and democratic control over decisions about basic social organization is weakened. To avoid aggravating inequality and worsening the position of those who are frequently already vulnerable in the reform process, three conditions need to be met.

First, conflicts of interests—between workers and entrepreneurs, for example–as well as the necessary tradeoffs that legal reforms often ential should be acknowledged openly, rather than hidden behind the veil of efficiency. This will allow countries to debate more openly the political and distributive choices that legal reforms involve. Second, donor countries and international financial institutions need to rethink the position that state "intervention" is usually or necessarily the enemy of economic development. Third, developing states need much more space, indeed they should be actively encouraged to accommodate distributive, equity and social concerns not only through social programmes and transfers but through the processes of legal and regulatory reform as well. This would allow greater attention to labour market concerns and environmental protection as well as to poverty alleviation and gender, racial and ethnic equity.

Chapter—18

An Agenda for Change

The world's growing population, combined with unsustainable production and consumption patterns, is putting increasing stress on air, land, water, energy, and other essential resources.

- Development strategies will have to deal with the combination of population growth ecosystem health, technology, and access to resources. Meeting the unmet need for family planning and reproductive health services should be part of national sustainable development strategies.
- The world needs to do a better job of forecasting the possible outcome of current human activities, including population trends, per capita resource use, and wealth distribution.

Protecting the atmosphere: The atmosphere is under increasing pressure from green house gases that threaten to change the climate and from chemicals that reduce the ozone layer. Governments need to:

- Modernize existing power system to gain energy efficiency and develop new and renewable energy sources.
- Promote national energy efficiency and emission standards and develop efficient, cost-effective, and less polluting mass transit systems.

Combating deforestation: Forests world-wide are threatened by uncontrolled degradation and conversion to other uses because of increasing human pressure.

- There is an urgent need to conserve and plant forests in developed and developing countries to maintain or restore the ecological balance and to provide for human needs.
- Governments need to work with business, scientists, local community groups, indigenous people, and the public to create long-term conservation and management policies for every forest region and watershed.

Sustainable agriculture and rural development: Hunger is already a constant threat to over 800 million people, while the world's ability to continue meeting growing demand for food and other agricultural products over the long term is uncertain. Soil erosion, salinization, waterlogging, and loss of soil fertility are increasing in all countries.

Agriculture has to meet rising needs mainly by increasing productivity, because most of the world's best croplands are already in use. At the same time further encroachment on land that is only marginally suitable for cultivation must be avoided.

- Sustainable agriculture and rural development will require major adjustments in agricultural, environmental, and economic policies in all countries and at the international level.

Conservation of biological diversity: The lost of the world's biological diversity continues, mainly from habitat destruction, over-harvesting, pollution, of foreign plants and animals (known and exotic). This decline in biodiversity is largely caused by human activity and represents a serious threat to our development.

- Develop national strategies to conserve and sustainably use biological diversity and to make these strategies part of overall national development efforts.
- Implement fair sharing of the benefits between providers and consumers of biological resources.
- Protect natural habitats. Promote the rehabilitation of damaged ecosystems.

Protecting and managing the oceans: Oceans are under increasing environmental stress from pollution over-fishing, and degradation of coastlines and coral reefs. About 70% of marine pollution comes from sources on land. Countries should commit themselves to control and reduce degradation of the marine environment. They should:

- Build and maintain sewage-treatment systems and avoid discharging sewage near shell fisheries, water intakes and bathing areas.
- Develop land-use practices that reduce run-off of soil and wastes to rivers and thus to the seas. Use environmentally less harmful pesticides and fertilizers.
- Control and prevent coastal erosion and silting due to land uses such as unplanned construction.

Protecting and managing fresh water: In many parts of the world there is widespread scarcity, gradual destruction, and increased pollution of freshwater resources. The causes include the inadequately treated sewage and industrial waste, loss of natural water catchment areas, deforestation and other chemicals into the water. The following approaches are key:

- The way to provide all people with potable water and basic sanitation is to adopt the approach "some for all rather than more for some." This approach can be achieved through low-cost services built and maintained at the community level.
- Nations need to identify and protect water resources and see that water is used on a sustainable basis. They need effective water pollution prevention and control programmes. There is a particular need for appropriate sanitation and waste-disposal technologies for low-income, high-density cities.

Chapter—19
Add Value, Go Global

Can Southern Firms Break into Export Markets?

The global economy has changed beyond recognition over the last decade. Widespread economic policy reform and in particular trade liberalisation have opened up new opportunities for developing countries. In poor countries, however, the consequences of trade liberalisation are not always positive. What can be private sector do to respond better and make the most of new trading opportunities? What factors have limited the impact of economic reforms on export performance?

Why have exports from poorer countries failed to increase more rapidly following trade liberalisation? What can be done to improve performance? Research on the response of firms in the private sector to economic reform can underpin new approaches to export promotion for poorer developing countries. For a long time, protective trade policies, poorly performing state-owned industries and state controls over the private sector were blamed for poor export performance in Africa and South Asia. Now that some of these problems have been remedied, other obstacles have come to light.

The effect of economic liberalisation and adjustment on the performance of poor countries has been cause for concern. Trade liberalisation should increase incentives to export and facilitate business enterprise by encouraging private ownership through privatisation and by attracting foreign investment. Macroeconomic stability ought to boost business confidence and performance. All these factors should promote exports, offsetting job and income losses caused by the closure or reorganisation of inefficient enterprises and industries yet, although some degree of reform and stability it is without export growth that was expected.

Trade reform and macroeconomic stability may be necessary conditions for improved export performance but by them are insufficient. The obstacles to improving export performance are numerous and there is no easy policy answer. The research programme examined export performance at three levels.

- **Regional:** how trade strategies should vary with skills and natural resource endowments
- **National:** factors influencing the export performance of manufacturing
- **Sectoral:** the performance of particular sectors of the economy.

The East Asian economies have shown that developing countries can complete successfully in global markets. For many, they provide a blueprint for economic growth applicable to many poor countries.

South Asia's comparative advantage lies in its abundant unskilled labour, while Africa's lies in its abundant natural resources. Different export promotion strategies are essential. South Asia's best prospectus are in labour-intensive manufacturing: the region's low level of exports would soar over the next decade if current obstacles to trade were reduced. Africa's exports could also increase but its biggest potential in primary products that need little educated labour and abundant natural resources.

Some African countries could also be substantial exporters of manufacturers, but their actual manufactured exports in most cases now fall far short. Comparing Ghana to Mauritius—one of Africa's most successful exporters of manufactured goods differences in firm-level efficiency are apparent. Mauritian firms have more capital per worker and use it more efficiently. Reducing trade barriers is not sufficient. Wages in Ghana would have to be substantially lower to offset low labour productivity.

Alternatively, labour productivity will have to be drastically improved if Ghanian firms are to compete successfully in export markets with wages at current levels.

Even when companies use capital and labour efficiently, poor infrastructure is a frequent stumbling products to export markets—an acute problem in landlocked countries and equally acute for manufacturers as research on Uganda clearly shows. What huts manufacturing exporters is being hit by the high cost of transporting their output to foreign markets and of transporting the materials they need from abroad. The cost penalties resulting from geography and poor infrastructure are far greater in Uganda than from high tariffs and other import restrictions.

Southern firms can still break into export markets, however. Developing—country firms do export to markets with exacting standards for product quality, reliability of delivery, and consumer safety. Two crucial aspects, however, are often overlooked:

- Non manufacturing sectors, such as tourism and horticulture, generate significant employment and offer opportunities for supplying increasingly sophisticated products. Although manufacturing is considered more attractive, certain areas of tourism and horticulture can be equally appealing.
- New export opportunities are created as southern producers establish closer links with foreign customers. Producers of labour-intensive products such as garments, horticulture and footwear frequently depend on large retailers and specialist international traders for designs, information about demand and technical support.

Supermarkets make key decisions about which fruit and vegetables to grow, how they should be produced and processed and which firms should be included in the business. Strategic decisions by international producers and retailers in the footwear industry have been crucial in developing new production locations such as Vietnam and Romania. Similarly, work on automotive components production in South Africa and India illustrates how global sourcing by the leading motor companies closes off some markets and opens up others. Export prospects can only be evaluated in the light of global restructuring in these industries.

Emphasising global linkages does not mean that developing countries are powerless in the face of global forces. Even in tightly-structured industries, there is scope for national policy and national strategy. Furthermore, there are important export sectors that are not structured in this way. Some tourism is dominated by large northern firms and is heavily import-dependent, but there is also enormous potential and national policy will be crucial in shaping the industry and its contribution to the economy as a whole.

For southern firms to break into export markets, certain issues must be addressed, especially in Africa. Some are recognised as important policy issues – investing in human capital and improving infrastructure for example. As one set of constraints are reduced – such as removing policy—induced distortions through trade liberalisation—another set takes precedence. In response to the integration of global markets, southern producers must join the global distribution chains to ensure markets for their exports.

These findings impose hard choices on developing countries. Should a firm allocate limited funds for investment in human capital or investment infrastructure? Future research might contribute by quantifying relative rates of return. On another level, countries may worry about the independence and autonomy of local producers if they are to join a global chain typically donated by northern companies. Rules regulate governmental trade and investment policies but who controls the global buyers and multinational companies whose decisions have such huge impacts on developing countries?

Chapter—20

Beyond Economics

Unless policymakers take a more all-round view of education, they risk sending their countries down the wrong path. Over the past decade, educational change in most countries has been driven by one imperative: survival in the global economy. This process has been particularly salient in the Asia-Pacific region following the drastic shock of the 1997 economic downturn. But in the current reform process, marked by speeding commercialization and economic preoccupations, other educational missions are being ignored, and countries risk paying a high price for their shortsightedness.

There's no denying that economic considerations are critical in today's world. Students have to acquire the knowledge and skills to survive and compete in the global economy, especially one which more than ever before prizes human capital. A high-quality labour force gives nations a cutting edge in global competition. Understandably, stressing economic returns in the current educational debate attracts private resources. But education has other functions that are the indispensable corollary of more balanced, equitable development. They deserve to be briefly explained.

The first is a social function: education has a role to play in facilitating social mobility and bringing about integration in often very diverse constituencies. It is at school that children learn how to form a broader set of relationships, to live together and become aware of belonging to teach us civic attitudes, to make us aware of our rights and responsibilities—in essence, to become responsible citizens. The task is fundamental in light of democracy's advance in so many countries over the past decade or so. Then there is education's cultural function. Developing creativity and aesthetic awareness, accepting other traditions and belief systems while valuing our own are all part of the path towards fulfilment. Finally, education is a goal in and of itself. Schools help children learn how to learn and play a pivotal role in transferring knowledge from one generation to the next. I believe that all these facets of learning are critical for the long-term prosperity of our societies. In our globalized, interdependent world, these functions take on a more international character. Everywhere, education has a role to play in eliminating racial and gender biases, promoting global common interests, moments for peace, and greater international understanding.

Rising above Short-Term Pressures to Strike a Harmonious Balance

While education is widely recognized as the spine of the learning society, the complexity lies in striking a balance between these various functions. The commercialization of education that we are witnessing the world over inevitably pushes schools, educators, parents and policymakers to pursue short-term, market-driven outcomes. Lawyers, bankers and businessmen have an increasingly high profile in educational debates. Following Southeast Asia's downturn in 1997, they were influential in changing the academic mindset. In little time, emphasis has shifted from academic achievement to developing communication skills, creativity, adaptability. In and of itself, this is not necessarily regrettable. The problem is that these skills are all perceived to be at the service of a supreme economic value.

Sounder research will be required to analyze and assess where the current trends are leading us. It is increasingly recognized, however, that unless economic growth is accompanied by good governance, a fair sharing of benefits, better social and environmental protection and attention to culture, it will, sooner or later, lead to unrest. It is through education that this broad spectrum of concerns can be nurtured. Policymakers who have taken stock of this holistic mission unfortunately represent a minority in today's educational debates and reforms. Their foremost challenge is to manage commercialization, to rise above short-term pressures and to take a more ethical stance towards education, a long-term strategic view.

Chapter—21
Finance Matters

Financial Liberalisation: Too Much Too Soon?

An efficient and stable financial system is important for economic growth and poverty reduction. The financial crises that have afflicted many countries in recent times have been a costly and painful reminder of the disastrous consequences for development of weak financial markets. The recurrence of financial crises, at both the international and national levels, and the adverse effect they have had on economic growth and poverty levels, have highlighted the need for a policy framework which addresses the inherent vulnerability of financial markets to systemic instability and failure.

Governments have always intervened in the financial sector and there are sound theoretical and practical reasons for doing so. Financial markets are characterised by problems of limited and unequal information, making them inherently imperfect and prone to failure. Financial regulation and supervision are therefore essential for efficient and stable financial market development. How should governments intervene? Have financial liberalisation and financial sector reform made financial systems more or less vulnerable to instability and systemic crises? How can the process be better managed? What is the best policy framework for supporting financial sector development in low-income countries.

Repression to Liberalisation

For many years, governments followed a policy of financial 'repression', which relied on fixing interest rates below market levels and controlling the allocation of credit. The economic distortions induced by these policies were considerable. Financial systems remained under-developed, lending patterns were inefficient and failed to achieve their distributional goals. Negative real interest rates led to low savings and encouraged capital flight. Macro-economic performance also deteriorated countries with large negative real interest rates experienced lower allocation efficiency and growth rates. In the state-owned banking sector, poor lending decisions (often politically influenced) and low repayment rates led to bank insolvency and large budgetary bailouts of depositors and creditors.

A growing awareness of the economic costs of financial 'repression' led to financial 'liberalisation' as the dominant policy paradigm over the past two decades. Initially, the relaxation of controls on interest rates was the focus for financial reform which was often triggered by a financial crisis. The relaxation of controls on the financial sector was often part of a more general policy shift towards liberalisation of the domestic economy and opening up to the international economy liberalisation soon broadened therefore beyond interest rate liberalisation, to include a wide range of measures constituting a programme of financial sector reform was adopted under World Bank sectoral or structural adjustment lending conditionalities, the key elements of which included privatisation of banks, entry of new domestic and foreign entrants into the banking sector, bank restructuring and recapitalisation, opening upto the capital account, strengthening bank regulation and supervision institutions.

Has Financial Liberalisation Worked

The period of financial liberalisation coincided with, or was soon followed by heightened financial instability, culminating in the dramatic financial crisis in East Asia in the second half of the 1990s. Clearly, financial liberalisation has not led to a smooth transition to a stable and efficient financial system. It would be wrong, however, to jump to the easy, but shallow, conclusion that financial liberalisation has 'failed'. Firstly, the fact that the period of increased systemic instability does not prove causality. Secondly, no process of change comes cheap: a reasoned assessment of the costs and benefits of the policy change is needed. And thirdly, what would have been the outcome without the policy change? Finally the impact of financial liberalisation will differ between countries, depending on each country's economic and institutional characteristics. The more relevant research issue, therefore, relates to the design and timing of context-specific policy measures, which will contribute to the development of an efficient and stable financial system. Could financial liberalisation have been managed better? If so, what policies are now needed? The commercial banks are the dominant component of the financial sector in low-income countries and are critical to the efficiency and stability of the financial system as a whole. Financial liberalisation was associated with a shift in prudential regulation from direct regulation of banks, by for example, regular site visits, to an indirect approach based on the monitoring of bank capital to ensure that it remained adequate in relation to the risk being taken. Additional regulatory measures are also necessary to restrain the activities of the privatised and other newly-established private banks. The regulatory and supervisory framework may also need to be extended to cover microfinance institutions which have developed significant deposit taking capacity.

Four main obstacles to efficient banking regulations are:

(a) information, contracting and monitoring problems,

(b) lack of supervisory personnel,

(c) high operational costs, and

(d) poor credibility and regulation of regulatory bodies. The appropriateness of various policy measures for dealing with these constraints are discussed and ranked in terms of their suitability for low-income countries. What are the implications of allowing microfinance institutions to offer a range of financing services beyond small-scale lending.

Too Much, Too Soon?

The experience with financial liberalisation reveals a strong correlation between liberalisation and financial crisis. This can be explained partly by the exposure of existing inefficiencies and distortions in the financial structure, and partly by a failure to develop a strong regulatory and supervisory framework, prior to liberalisation. Weakness in the initial conditions affect the ability of the privatised banks and new market entrants, to operate on broadly commercial principles. Borrowers are often unable to service their loans, due to poor quality lending and high interest rates. Liberalisation of the capital account increases the inflow of foreign capital, but at the same time threatens that stability of the financial institutions by increasing the exchange rate and domestic lending risks.

The existing regulatory and supervisory system may be unsuited to a market-based environment. Consequently, across-the-board 'big-bang' financial liberalisation and financial sector reform increase the likelihood of systemic crisis, where the institutional and human resource environment is weak. Much of the blame for post-liberalisation financial crisis lies, therefore, with the scale and sequencing of financial reform. What is needed is a more gradual and considered approach to financial liberalisation, which recognises that institutional strengthening, especially in the regulation and supervision capacity, is a prerequisite for creating a more efficient and stable financial sector which can contribute fully to achieving economic growth and poverty reduction in developing countries.

Chapter—22

Literacy Gaining too Slowly

In the past five decades, the number of adults who can read has increased by about 1.8 billion world-wide – a net growth of some 1,20,000 people a day. This continuing improvement in global literacy from 56 per cent of the population in 1950 to about 74 per cent today represents encouraging progress. But it also hides troubling disparities between industrial and developing nations and between men and women.

In 1970, some 94 per cent of adults over age 15 were considered literate in industrial countries, compared with only 45 per cent in the Third World. Since then, literacy rates in the developing countries have gained ground impressively, climbing to 65 per cent. Unfortunately, that still leaves 1.4 billion illiterate adults worldwide. With population having grown even faster than literacy over most of the past three decades, the absolute number of people who cannot read is greater now than it was in the early 1960s.

As education programmes proliferated in the developing world between 1995 and 2000, literacy finally began to gain on population growth, and the total number of illiterates world wide fell by 2.4 million – the first time the number has actually declined. At the rate of improvement, however, it would take 3,000 years for the number of illiterates to approach zero. Furthermore, as the income gap between rich and poor nations is now widening rather than narrowing, maintaining even this rate of improvement may be difficult.

The disparity between male and female literacy is pervasive, cutting across economic and regional lines. In 1970, about 70 per cent of the world's men were able to read, but only 54 per cent of the women. By 1990, both sexes had increased in overall literacy but the gap between the two had narrowed only slightly by 2 percentage points. At this rate, it would take more than 200 years for women to be as literate as men.

Even more disturbing is the fact that in some areas, the gender gap has actually widened. In Africa, while women's literacy climbed from 11 per cent in 1962 to about 30 per cent in 1985, the rate for men increased from 26 to 56 per cent during the same period; thus the gender gap increased from 15 percentage points to 26. Since 1985 however, African women have closed the gap slightly.

Illiteracy in industrial countries, while affecting a diminishing percentage of the population, appears to constitute a growing social problem. Because an increasing proportion of all jobs in these economics demand some facility in reading and writing, those who lack these skills are often mired in chronic unemployment and poverty

In the Third World, literacy is not only a key factor in economic productivity but is a basic—though often disregarded—factor in the vicious cycle wherein uncontrolled population growth hastens environmental degradation, leading to still more intractable poverty. Efforts to stabilize population growth are unlikely to succeed without fundamental improvements in the status of women—including their rights and access to education. Closing the literacy gap between men and women may thus be a significant measure of progress in human development.

Regionally, there are large differences in literacy. Both overall and in terms of women's literacy, Africa is the most deprived of the continents. In 1990, less than a quarter of the adult population was literate in six countries in the world—all of them in Africa. In 19 nations, 17 of them in Africa, the lifetime total schooling averaged less than one year for each adult. And in Burkina Faso, Djibouti, and Somalia, where fewer than one woman in five could read, it averaged less than three months.

The functional importance of literacy to economic growth was formally recognized at a World Congress on Illiteracy in

1965, which gave impetus to the establishment of numerous national programmes. Subsequent statistical surveys demonstrate a high correlation between literacy rates and income. In real per capita income, the 20 wealthiest countries in the world in 1990 included 18 of the 20 nations with the highest adult literacy scores. The only notable exception was Ireland, which ranked near the top in literacy but had modest per capita income, albeit higher than in most developing countries.

Conversely, the greatest impoverishment is generally found in countries with lowest per capita gross domestic product (GDP) in 1990, the average adult had slightly more than one year of schooling.

These general observations are confirmed by studies showing that when literacy is increased in a given country, productivity also rises. A study of 88 countries found that a 20 to 30 per cent increase in literacy produced gains of 8 to 16 per cent in GDP. Another study concluded that "about a fifth of income inequality could be explained by educational inequality."

Beyond economic motives, several other forces have propelled the movement that has led, during this century from a world in which a minority of people could read to one in which three of every four people can. At the 1985 International Conference on Adult Education in Paris, literacy was identified as a fundamental human "right to learn".

The idea of literacy as a means to liberation has spread widely, and has clearly been a factor in the global movement toward democracy.

With few exceptions, low literacy is associated not only with greater poverty but with greater likelihood of political and social instability—resulting in still further sapping of national assets as resources are directed toward military security rather than social investment. A telling measure of this phenomenon is the ratio of soldiers to teachers, which is far higher in countries with low literacy and high poverty. It may be noteworthy that of 160 countries surveyed, the two with the highest solder-teacher ratios where every one the U.S. government perceived a need for military intervention during the past three years; Somalia and Iraq.

Chapter—23

Who is Responsible for Corruption in Aid?

World Bank President James Wolfensohn's pronouncement that the 'cancer' of corruption seriously undermines development and will not be tolerated in future. Bank funded projects prompt one to ask: where and when did this corruption originate? How much corruption is acceptable to the World Bank and donor community? For many years the World Bank tended to ignore or discount the significance of corruption in its operations. Donor agencies in general seem to have a very high tolerance for the misuse of their money. Now that the Bank, the UK system, and bilateral agencies are under growing pressure to improve their performance, they are seeking ways to limit the corrupt use of aid money. For the moment, there is little or no evidence that they have any idea of how to go about the task.

One of the main reasons for the disappointing performance of structural adjustment programmes is the misuse of donor money, including systematic corruption. An extreme example is Tanzania's import support programme, which allowed local manufacturers and traders to import raw materials and finished goods. An increasing number of companies, both private and parastatal, began to abuse the system. They stopped paying counterpart funds. Import duty and sales tax were not paid on imports. Neither the Treasury nor the commercial banks had the administrative capacity or the integrity to handle large volumes of free foreign exchange, but the donors ignored the problem. Only when the scandalous behaviour of the banks, the Treasury and the Minister of Finance had reached epic proportions, fuelling inflation and completely derailing the budgetary process, did the World Bank and other donors finally pull the plug on import support.

In December 1996, the IMF started disbursing US $ 240 million enhanced structural adjustment loan, but to date not one private or parastatal company has been put in receivership for the hundreds of millions of donor dollars which went astray via import support. This casual approach to large-scale corruption has been the norm among donors.

Some bilateral donors have cut the number of countries which they assist, and eradicated funds to those remaining. To increase aid effectiveness some of them have also reduced the number of sectors they support per country. Add to this the tendency for the whole donor community to move into new activities at the same time, and you have a recipe for too much aid chasing too little 'absorptive capacity' in the countries of concentration which include Tanzania, Uganda and Kenya. Pressure to spend has led to unbelievable overfunding in certain sectors. Well known examples are NGO's, many of which are created with the sole objective of embezzling donor money.

With the coming of political pluralism, a growing volume of aid money has been channelled into 'governance' activities. The disadvantages of governance from the donor perspective are that donors have little experience in this field, and the amounts of money which can be disbursed, compared to the amount of administrative work involved, are relatively trivial.

Aid has served to encourage the establishment of a whole range of corrupt activities in 'civil society' to add to those which already existed in the state apparatus. Many of those managing the corruption are recent migrants from the state sector, or straddle both public and private sectors. The politically acceptable employment of more local personnel as desk officers has served to increase the rate of corruption. The chances of being caught or punished are minimal. The few genuine local change-agents are crowded out by the charlatans and opportunists. The imperative to disburse at all costs makes it very difficult for donors to adequately monitor or evaluate the quality of their assistance, since it would put the agencies in a poor light if they were seen to be supporting non-performing and corrupt activities. Thus, as has generally been the case, the donors pretend that their assistance is being well used, and are even prepared to deny well founded allegations of the misuse of project funds.

The new aid activities discussed above account for a relatively small proportion at total aid flows, however. The basic issue is the amount of uncontrolled corruption which still characterises the World Bank and other donors' more traditional project, programme, and financial support. Here too one finds projects of ever growing magnitude, as the big spending goes on. The continued availability of donor money is the major determinant of the volume of aid, not performance, structural reform or impact on 'target groups'. Although further project aid cannot be justified on the basis of past performance, it continues to be a major form of aid delivery by both the World Bank and other donor agencies.

The picture which emerges is that of an oppressed people largely at the mercy of an incompetent and corrupt state apparatus. The role of aid in helping to create and reproduce this lamentable state of affairs is worth exploring. Unfortunately, the report does not mention corruption in aid. If corruption has become one of the major international issues of modern times, it would hardly be surprising to find that the virus has already infected and is spreading within the major agencies.

If countries with as much corruption as Tanzania, Uganda, and Kenya can continue to enjoy billions of dollars of aid every year, it is not because they have demonstrated their ability to use aid wisely. But the donors are not well placed to extol the virtues of transparency and accountability which they do not practise themselves. To address the question of corruption in aid, the World Bank and other agencies will have to take a long look at their own role in creating the problem which they now propose to cure.

Chapter—24

Will Education Go to Market?

The World Trade Organisation has launched processes that could open up to competition the expanding and highly protected world market in education. What issues are at stake? Most of us see education as first and foremost a public service which is responsible for providing young people with instruction. For investors looking for somewhere to put their money it is also an annual budget of $1,000 billion worldwide, a sector employing 50 million people, and above all a billion potential customers in the form of students.

The decision to extend to services the liberalization of international trade which previously applied to commodities was taken in 1994. The Genral Agreement on Trade in Services (GATS) which was signed in April of that year included education on the list of services to be liberalised. To stay outside the scope of this agreement a country's education system must be completely financed and administered by the state, which is no longer the case anywhere. However, each country can still decide freely what commitments it wants to make, and especially which educational sectors it wants to expose to market forces. The New Zealand government, for example, has decided to open up to outside competition the whole private education sector, from primary to university level.

So far, New Zealand is an exception, but that situation is likely to change. Part 4 of the GATS agreement ("Progressive liberalisation") requires that fresh negotiations should be held by the end of 2000 at the latest, and should be directed to "the elimination of the adverse effects on trade in services of measures as a means of providing effective market access". At the Geneva headquarters of the World Trade Organisation (WTO), far from the headlines and the demonstrators, work still goes on. But independently of the WTO and national policies, a number of factors are driving educational systems towards "communication".

Pressures for Change

First, education is a rapidly-growing sector in which governments are finding it harder and harder to satisfy demand, above all in higher education. Between 1985 and 1992, the number of students in higher education rose about 26 per cent—from 58.6 to 73.7 million. Meanwhile, public spending on education has tended to stagnate over the past 15 years (5-6 per cent of GDP in rich countries and 4 per cent elsewhere).

In view of this dearth of public spending, parents and students are increasingly looking to private education for a solution. In the United States, every episode of violence in a state school and every scandal that rocks official school systems gives a boost to "home schooling", where children no longer attend school and are taught at home.

Traditional public education is also coming in for strong criticism. Employers complain it is not geared to their needs and is not flexible enough. Under pressure from economic interests, a process of "deregulating" education systems has begun. The growing independence of schools is encouraging them to look for alternative sources of funding, ranging from sponsorship to full management by private companies and including many kinds of partnerships between schools and firms. The time for out-of-school education has come... the liberalisation of the educational process thereby made possible will lead to control by education service providers who are more innovative than the traditional structures.

The development and spread of information and communication technologies on a massive scale make possible the development of paid distance learning, using multimedia and the internet for tutorials, examinations, etc.

Secondary and primary education is also affected. More and more paying internet sites bill themselves as alternatives to state schools or traditional private schools. The computer screen takes over from the teacher, for a fee of around $2,250 a year.

The WTO secretariat set up a working group in 1998 to look at prospectus for more liberalised education. Its report pointed to the rapid growth of distance learning and noted the increasing number of partnerships between educational institutions and private firms.

Education for Export

Some 350 U.S. experts on international trade in services, including 170 businessmen and women, gathered at the U.S. Commerce Department in Washington on October 16, 1998 to draw up recommendations for the U.S. negotiators at the WTO. The purpose of the meeting, called Services 2000, was to look at how the U.S. government should continue to support the efforts of American business to take competitive advantage in foreign markets". The U.S. currently controls about 16 per cent of the world market in services. Its services exports have more than doubled in the past 10 years and now cover 42 per cent of the non-services trade deficit.

The United States is also the world's leading exporter of educational services, and a working group at the Services 2000 conference paid special attention to this sector. It concluded that the sector "needs the same degree of transparency, transferability and interchangeability, mutual recognition, and freedom from undue regulation or restraints and barriers that the United States acknowledges on behalf of other service industries". The report said that three points should be at the centre of WTO negotiations about education.

Firstly, there should be a free flow of electronic information and means of communication, nationally and internationally. Secondly, the negotiators should tackle "barriers and other restrictions that limit or prevent the provision of educational and training services across countries and internationally." They were also to deal with obstacles to the transferability of degrees and diplomas.

Fighting for Market Share

The U.S. demands are backed by most countries of the APEC (Asia-Pacific Economic Cooperation) zone. In a note in October 1999, the Australian delegation to the WTO said it would be "encouraging all members to make expanded commitments in all sectors, even the ones that have proved difficult in both regional and multilateral services negotiations", particularly education.

South Korea took a similar position. At a meeting of ministers of human resources from APEC countries that it hosted in September 1997, the Seoul government put out a memorandum which clearly stated its vision of education as a tool of economic competition.

"The emphasis on education for itself or on education for good members of a community without a large emphasis on preparation for future work is no longer appropriate. Such a view of education and work cannot be justified in a world where economic development is emphasized.

"At present, in many economies, the education systems do not sufficiently reflect labour market conditions. Their inflexible and inefficient education systems could not meet the new economic environmental challenges." So education should be made more "flexible", i.e. be deregulated and liberalized. In particular, "School systems should be established to allow all students to study what they are interested in" and "employers, with school educators, should share the role of educating students".

Some think resistance to liberalizing education will come from Europe, especially France. "The future WTO negotiations cannot call in question France's tradition of public service in the field of education and health," stressed a report on the WTO.

Chapter—25
Living with Leviathan

In the year 2015, there will be mega-cities with more than 8 million inhabitants—22 of them in Asia. How will they cope? Humanity is about to set a new record. Nearly two-thirds of the planet's population will be living in cities by 2025, UN population experts say. Until now, rural people have outnumbered city-dwellers.

World population, according to the same projections, will top eight billion in 25 years' time, including five billion in cities. The increase will be particularly spectacular in the cities of the developing world, whose total population will double to four billion. We are going to see an unprecedented exodus of people from rural areas.

The demographers' predictions are only tentative of course. But the flow of people into megacities in developing countries is well under way. Several sociological changes are behind it.

Cities used to need muscle-power for the jobs they provided, the experts point out. But today they no longer attract people just because of their economic potential. There's plenty of evidence that they can go on steadily attracting people even when the job-generating sectors are in bad shape or disappearing.

People no longer move to urban centers because they are fairly sure to find work. They do so because they want to leave the countryside where there are too many people tilling the land and because they hope to leave poverty behind. Rightly or wrongly, the city seems to offer progress and freedom, a vision of opportunity, an irresistible lure.

The result is that both inside and outside cities, there are more and more squatters and poor housing. Urbanization in the developing world differs from that in the industrialized countries, in "the speed of the process, the growth of poverty, the extent of urban sprawl and the expansion of the informal economy".

How are the authorities in the developing world's urban areas responding to such "invasions"? In today's deregulated world, the trend is to question the very idea of providing the general population with basic urban services, most observers note. For want of resources, cities in developing countries are increasingly abandoning their public service function.

China is still an exception to this in several ways. Officials there, in a context of rigid planning—though this has eased in recent years—are trying to prevent the influx of more rural migrants than the city economies can cope with, as the example of Shanghai shows. Can such a policy, which works fairly well for the moment, survive the political and economic hangs under way?

At the other end of the scale is Lagos (Nigeria), whose expansion is chaotic. About 200 slums have sprung up in this African city. Every now and then, one of them is bulldozed without notice and without heed for its inhabitants. But Lagos survives thanks to the vibrant ingenuity of its millions of citizens. Another revealing city is Jakarta, where the authorities themselves have joined in frantic property speculation. As a result of this speculation, more than 4.5 million people have been evicted from their homes in the last 30 years, with little compensation, to make possible the construction of high-rise blocks, which sometimes stand empty.

How do the original inhabitants of a city react to the massive influx of people from outside? In more and more cities, you see smart neighbourhoods protected by guards—called "fortress-cities". In these fortified enclaves, built partly in response to real or imagined lack of security, the roads, sewage system, schools and other community services are private. Outside them, public areas have been abandoned to the least fortunate members of the society and the infrastructure there is crumbling or inadequate. The middle and poorer classes also defend themselves in their own neighbourhoods. One surprising case can be found in the satellite cities just outside Brasilia, where iron railings protect the houses, from fancy villas to the humblest shack.

Will the mega-cities of the 21st century be made up of islands of "social tribes" – "anticities" of walled enclaves, whose wealthy residents refuse to pay taxes to provide facilities for the city's less fortunate inhabitants? Will cities still integrate their inhabitants?

"The existence of a slum means the authorities have failed," says the World Bank. The bank encourages projects where the state and the private sector join hands to help the less fortunate buy plots of land in areas with an infrastructure. Other experts say the "anti-social" aspects of globalization should be blamed. They would like to see the big cities of the next century return to their original function as a crossroads and a meeting-place.

Chapter—26

Myths and Illusions

The tide of precarity is rising steadily, so that people who have never been poor no longer regard poverty as a distant prospect but as one so close that it could engulf them at any moment.

In 1989, the fall of the Berlin Wall was rightly welcomed because it marked the collapse of a system that provided a degree of equality but rejected freedom. Today there is a strong possibility that the system gradually spreading all over the world—a kind of neo-liberal fundamentalism—may also collapse. In its obsession with freedom, vital though freedom is, this fundamentalism disregards equality, a term which should not be regarded here in purely static and statistical terms, but as something dynamic and ethical. Equality can only be truly practised in a context of social solidarity or to borrow from the vocabulary of the French Revolution of fraternity.

On the one hand, we have a world that is immensely rich in resources, possibilities, knowledge and experience; its constituent societies are freer and more dynamic than ever. There is an extraordinary potential for everyone to live a better life. But at the same time, new and ever higher walls are being built both between peoples and between social groups within individual countries. We are experiencing a travesty of development, which is creating a world bipolarized into extremes of wealth and poverty.

The most common reactions to this disastrous situation are very often the result of two misapprehensions. The first can only be described as ideological or doctrinaire since it is not based on the facts as they can be observed. It says that since the dominant system of values and things is by definition more than satisfactory, the persistence of impoverishment is merely a temporary blip. Enough time has elapsed, however, for us to see that this is not the case, including in countries where this system has been part of the established order for more than a century. One statistic is particularly eloquent. In just over 30 years, world production has approximately doubled, but the gap has more than doubled between the income of the 20 per cent of world's people living in the richest countries and the income of the world's poorest 20 per cent, according to the United Nations Development Programme.

The second misapprehension stems from another form of blindness and illusion, namely the belief that poverty can be regarded exclusively as a moral issues, as if it had no other kind of implications for those who are not poor. Globalization is, however, a two-way process. It enables the countries of the North to export their values and their paradigms as well as their goods and capital to the countries of the South, but it also makes them much more vulnerable to the backlash of crises that afflict these countries. Even in the North, the cult of competitiveness is undermining situations once considered extremely stable. The tide of precarity is rising steadily, so that people who have never been poor no longer regard poverty as a distant prospect but as one so close that it could engulf them at any moment.

Because of inadequate socio-economic development, the extraordinary upsurge of democracy over the past 30 years remains a very fragile process, and there is a risk that the trend may be reversed. When hunger, disease and ignorance prevail, citizens' participation in decision-making becomes either non-existent or a mere charade. Democratic institutions become empty shells, representational bodies existing in form only and devoid of real significance.

Social divisions caused by economic distortions exacerbate the failures of democracy which in turn pose serious threats to civil order within countries and to peace between nations. It is high time to face these obvious facts.

Chapter—27

Solving the Unemployment Problem by Looking Beyond the Job

If you had a job, you worked; if you didn't, you didn't. Having a job meant being employed by an organization in a clearly-defined and stable occupational role, with duties, hours, rates of pay and promotion all more or less standardized. But the job—in that meaning of the word—is a social invention, and a fairly recent one.

The job—the kind that you had, or hoped to get—became a central fixture of life. Its importance was great because it served many needs: For managers and efficiency experts, job assignments were the key to assembly-line manufacturing. For union organizers, jobs protected the rights of workers. For political reformers, standardized civil service positions were the essence of good government. Jobs provided an identify to immigrants and recently-urbanized farm workers. They provided a sense of security for individuals and an organizing principle for society.

Jobs functioned in so many ways that it is surprising how many organizations are now opting for other ways to define and manage work. The second job shift is underway. Its emergence can be seen in the increasing use of temporary and part-time workers and contracted-out services, the changing relationships between workers and management, the growing popularity of self-employment and small business. Indeed, "de-jobbing" is proceeding at such a pace that many economists, management experts and futurists are now talking freely about the end of the job. Bridges predicts that the job as we now know it will disappear entirely—replaced by new kinds of flexible work assignments in post-job organizations—and be remembered only as a quaint artefact of the industrial age.

One reason for the change in work is the economic rules of the survival game among organizations that employ workers. To stay successful in today's hi-tech consumer economy, businesses have had to re-model themselves into what some experts call "agile companies" – ones that are able to respond quickly to conditions in ever-changing, fragmenting, competitive markets.

The "knowledge worker", whose work involves not simply doing something, but also applying theoretical or analytical skills. Such workers are replacing the industrial labourer as the dominant part of the workforce—and their productive activities are likely to be organized and structured much differently from those of their assembly-line predecessors.

De-jobbing as a result of new technology or the emergence of a service economy is a phenomenon that gets a lot of attention these days; but it is not the whole story. At all levels of society, people are improvising livelihoods that do not fit the industrial-era model. Immigrants to the developed countries, often unable to find steady jobs, nevertheless find places in the new landscape by being mobile, flexible, resourceful and imaginative: they moonlight, work part-time, share jobs, start small businesses. Their lives are often extremely difficult, but they are also instructive to those of us who believe you either have a job or you're out of luck.

It is too early to evaluate the implications of this multifaceted transformation of work, or to dismiss it as simply good or bad. Nevertheless, one cannot deny that it is taking place, and will bring about dramatic social changes.

On the downside, the job shift is causing great hardships for many workers and their families. It poses serious challenges to policy-makers, political activists and labour leaders. The basic question appears to be whether the key to global employment-development strategy is to play "catch-up"–trying to bring millions of people around the world into jobs in industries and the public sector; or to play "leapfrog" – creating new forms of employment.

The proposal to generate more employment in agriculture, for example, is based on new demand for agricultural exports from developing countries. The policies designed to make the most of this opportunity include measures to upgrade technology, raise productivity, ensure the supply of essential inputs, establish marketing and distribution channels, create links between agriculture and industry, and cater to export markets.

The issue of part-time work, another kind of employment that is seriously undervalued in the traditional industrial – era job mindset. Part-time work may not offer much at this point to developing countries, where many people are underemployed and wages are low, but it can be of great help in more advanced economies. And it is likely to be a big part of the global work picture in the years ahead.

A certain agility may also be necessary in agriculture, particularly in countries that for many years have depended heavily on producing commodities such as sugar for export as a means of generating income and employment. As Northern laboratories develop non-agricultural substitutes for many of these commodities—and this is already beginning to happen—the bottom may fall out of "monoculture" economies, only economic, but will have long-run political implications as communities attempt to reorganize themselves in response to the changed conditions. It is, therefore, in the interest of raw materials exporters to closely monitor current trends in biotechnology and the use of genetic resources and modify their internal policies in anticipation of potential long-term effects."

This calls for flexibility and an ability to get information and to act on it. Government officials, development workers, community leaders and individuals will, in some respects, all have to be "knowledge workers" if they are to keep ahead of global change. Jobs are going to be created not just by putting people to work, but by finding—or creating—new niches where they can be productive.

It is still possible to talk about jobs for all, and to resist the assumption made by many economists that high levels of unemployment are now inevitable. But, as we move ahead into the global information economy, we may be moving back into an older conception of the job, and seeing it again as something you do, rather than as something you have—or that has you.

Chapter—28

Policy Researchers and Policy Makers

Never the Twain Shall Meet?

In every corner of the planet, researchers are gathering and analyzing information on vital issues of sustainable development. But how do they know that their findings will actually be used in policy decisions that create positive change? Researchers and decision makers see the world, and their roles in it, in very different ways. What creates this divide between the two communities and what can be done to bridge the gap?

'Demand-side' Challenges: Policy in the Making

By its nature, the policy making process constrains decision makers from effectively expressing demands for research. Rigorous research requires a clear definition of a problem and the variables to be measured. But the objectives of government policies and programmes tend to be loosely defined and even contradictory. Many decisions are reached through a multilateral bargaining process in which it is difficult to obtain consensus on anything more than broad statements of principle. These bargains might break down if the costs and trade-offs involved were exposed by a research project.

Inertia and more urgent priorities mean that governments tend to think about changing policies only when time and funding have run out. At that point, it is too late for research. Furthermore, it is only after a programme has been established and a clientele created that an effective demand exists for research. For these reason, policy implementation tends to precede rather than follow research.

Even if there is a need for research, there may not be a single agency request advice, there is no guarantee that it will turn to be the appropriate audience for the results (e.g. a study done for the ministry of education might find that student performance would be improved by better nutrition).

Finally, governments are often afflicted with too much information, which senior policy makers have little time to absorb.

'Supply Side' Challenges of Academic Research

Problems also exist in the research community that supplies information and analysis. University research usually takes a long time to yield results. It is often highly critical, without suggestions for action, but fitting the self-image of many academics a gadflies. In academia, a state of conflicting views and information is normal. But potential clients find their confidence undermined when two studies reach opposite conclusions.

Academics often search for general laws and patterns that reveal phenomena of greater theoretical and long run importance than highly specific observations. Policy makers, however, want answers to the specific problems they face, even if such "small" problems do not interest researchers.

While policy makers tend to emphasize distributional concerns (i.e winners and losers) and the number of people affected, economists--frequent advisors to government—emphasize efficiency and financial costs and benefits. Owing partly to the vagueness of many programme goals, policy makers tend to assess performance in terms of inputs rather than improvements in health). They also weigh losses more heavily than gains, since "a policy that hurts five people and helps five, produces five enemies and five ingrates".

Finally, the issue of compensation is critical to policy makers; for economists it is usually an afterthought. Economists tend to find a solution satisfactory if, in theory, the losers could be compensated. To push a policy change through, policy makers must usually ensure that they will be compensated, and have mechanisms to do so.

Impact Down The Road

The gap between demand and supply for research appears rather large. But this view may be too pessimistic, mainly because it uses narrow definitions of research and policy impact. Research is more than a set of data and policy impact may accumulate imperceptibly but with real effect over many years. The contribution of social science research is perhaps less in proposing specific solutions to well-defined problems, than in defining the problems and providing an array of concepts and methods for analysis.

Problem definition can take many forms. It can mean detecting problems from patterns in data, such as a trend toward worsening income distribution. It can also change the way society thinks about issues. Largely because of research, the informal sector now tends to be seen as a potential force for development, rather than a symptom of backwardness.

The most significant contribution of social science research may be in generating ideas and ideologies, which history shows can be very powerful.

What to Do?

How, then, can researchers and the agencies that sponsor them increase the social relevance and impact of research? Since both the problem-solving and the conceptual impacts are important, research programmes a should be designed to provide both by developing an understanding of basic behavioural relationships and a thorough knowledge of the data. This can then be tapped to provide short-term policy advice.

Donors have an important role to play in supporting theoretical research, although they are sometimes reluctant to do so. The distinction between "theoretical" and "empirical" is in no sense equivalent to "useless" and "useful". A plausible, verifiable theory about how farmers respond to increases in crop prices, or savings to changes in interest rates, is of obvious relevance to poverty and can be very useful.

Greater attention should go to publicizing findings and donors should be prepared to finance conferences, books, working papers, abstracts and the like. Researchers should convey their findings in language intelligible to practitioners, putting themselves into policy makers' shoes when doing so. Among the recommendations made by successful policy advisors are the following.

- Learn about the history of the issue by researching previous arguments, interest groups, areas of disagreement and data gaps;
- Get into the debate early before positions harden;
- Explain which groups will be affected by the proposed measures and suggest ways to compensate those negatively affected;
- Do not propose measures that are technically optimal but too complex or costly for an agency to administer; and
- Keep it simple. Emphasize the decision at hand, the underlying problem, and options to solve it. Minimize methodology, jargon and equations.

In the research domain, there is no single recipe for policy impact. Luck and persistence, along with good science, are vital ingredients.

Chapter—29

Employment and Poverty Alleviation

Today the key socio-economic problem is large-scale unemployment. Spreading joblessness brings many other problems in its wake. It erodes national incomes and living standards, aggravating the already grindingly difficult job of promoting development and alleviating poverty. Joblessness also raises government budget deficits, increasing macro-economic instability while soaking up investment for productive capital expenditure, education, training and relief aid. And joblessness ruins lives and communities by depriving people of the dignity and satisfaction that comes with earning one's keep and making a contribution to the well-being of family and society.

Theories about how best to nurture development (and thus create jobs) have shifted considerably over the last decade. The state role has evolved, in the minds of many, from being a source of relief for the problems of unemployment, poverty and underdevelopment, to being a fundamental cause of these problems through the distorting impact of its intervention on the market.

However, the more market oriented philosophy that grew up during the 1990s has yet to provide convincing solutions in practice at least not on a grand scale, and especially not in terms of job creation as the present jobless economic recovery demonstrates.

The weakness of the current recovery and past approaches to economic development can be traced to the failure to consider employment as the predominant means of promoting growth and alleviating poverty. In policy circles it has too long been an almost ignored priority.

Current trends thus bode poorly, particularly as unemployment rates soar. In light of the circumstances, we need to begin re-examining some of the fundamental questions—if only to find out what has gone wrong with the answers.

Minimum Wage?

Let's begin with wages. With corporate restructuring in full force on a global scale, are low wage rates required to raise employment and maximize profits? A top manager of a multinational consumer electronics group certainly thinks so; he likened the perfect factory to a ship "so that we could move it around the world to where labour was cheapest". Perhaps, but this bottom-line emphasis on unit labour costs ignores at least two other factors; namely, that higher wages can act as a screen to select more productive workers and that higher wages translate into better productivity via improved worker nutrition, increased consumption and a generally healthier quality of life.

If higher wages bring these benefits (and it is an open question) should government insist that there be a minimum wage rate? Neo-classical economists tend to respond "no", assuming that a higher wage rate puts money into the pockets of some low wage workers while forcing many others out of work because companies cannot afford to pay them.

Technology Transfer

The impact of technology is another area in need of study. Technological innovation is usually labour-saving and tends to originate in industrialized countries, moving toward developing countries like India, Pakistan where labour tends to be low cost and abundant. Would it therefore make sense to slow down or somehow restrict technology transfer, especially to development markets, in the interest of preserving employment?

The answer here is clearly—no. Historical evidence abundantly demonstrates that attempts to retard technological progress bring about greater poverty and lower growth. Technology, in fact, is at the heart of the new endogenous growth theory which is very much in vogue among development economists today. Slowing down or inhibiting technology transfer would certainly dash many countries' development hopes and aggravate poverty. However, the relationship between technology, development, employment and poverty alleviation is not without its complications.

In the 1980s, the buzzword among development specialists was "appropriate technology", i.e., small-scale and labour-intensive technologies that would increase productive output while allowing an equilibrium solution to be found such that the ratio of the productivity of labour to that of capital is proportional to their relative prices. The conditions for this "small is beautiful" approach to technology tended to be best met in agricultural production. However, where manufacturing industry is concerned, the small-is-beautiful approach floundered badly when the only viable technological alternatives proved to be highly capital-intensive.

Development Gap

A wide gap has emerged between developing countries with an inward focus (which tended to be protectionist and pursue policies of import substitution) and those with an outward focus and a policy of pursuing export-led growth. Competing in international markets requires technology that is as good as or better than that found in advanced, industrialized nations. Small, therefore, is not beautiful in the global manufacturing economy where product standards are high and the elasticity of substitution between labour and capital is very limited.

The drive to obtain state-of-the-art technology thus leads to a policy conundrum: it is a pre-condition for success in manufactured exports, but the impulse to compete successfully in this most lucrative sector speeds up the transfer of technology from the developed to the developing world, thus reinforcing the bias toward labour saving equipment in developing countries and accelerating a process that is seen as a source of job loss in the industrialized countries.

Technology and Jobs

Before concluding that modern technology transfer is inimical to employment in developing countries, we have to distinguish clearly between technology's static and dynamic consequences. In a static sense, it is true that highly capital-intensive export industries may not create much employment on a net basis, but the dynamic effects of technology transfer do contribute to economic growth. And growth, in turn, generates multiplier effects in the form of demand, which stimulates ancillary production activities (like food processing or consumer goods) that rely on more labour-intensive technologies.

The problem is that the diffusion and application of technology on a global scale blurs the categories of international product specialization and creates a much more competitive and conflict-prone international environment.

For example, we have already seen the Asian Tigers move from producing goods such as textiles and processed food to producing hi-tech and value-added consumer durables. This advance is only possible due to the growth of human capital (facilitated by investment and higher incomes) and it leaves production of textiles to other industrializing countries, like Indonesia, the Philippines and now China. But the dynamic comes at the expense of jobs in industrialized regions, like the US and the EC, which lost more than a quarter of their work force in textiles during the 1980s. Inspite of job losses, advanced countries continue to produce textiles, notwithstanding major differences in the hourly wage rates for spinning and weaving and the fact that essentially the same hi tech equipment is being used in most production centres

Protectionism

What has happened in textiles is happening in other industrial sectors (automobiles, for example) as well. The intense market competition is proving to be a source of trade conflicts, and possibly protectionism, as jobs come under increasing pressure.

For many workers and managers, the benefits of foreign direct investment look increasingly like a zero-sum game for employment, and there is a real risk that the tenuous link between overall growth and employment will break down altogether. It is hardly surprising that we are already seeing negatively affected workers and local businesses clamouring for protection in advanced countries.

Governments Role

The concerned governments are supposed to carry out much of this research. The three initial lines of inquiry flow from three reasonable assumptions about the future.

- First, increase in welfare and consumption subsidies are out; investments in training and human capital are in. How can investments in human capital be directed to positive employment effects? Is it perhaps not time to explore more fully benefit schemes targeting the unemployed and the unskilled poor providing them with the type of subsidies that would enhance their human capital, improve their health and productivity through better nutrition and preventive medicine, and restore the dignity of holding a job?
- Second, given the quasi-inevitability of increased automation in manufacturing, how can other sectors (particularly agriculture and services) be employment creation?
- Third, given the inevitable pressures of work and productivity in the global economy, what sort of alternative institutional arrangements need to evolve with respect to industrial relations, employment and work conditions?

Finding answers to these and other questions will require no small amount of new thinking, but parochialism or a failure of imagination would be fatal flaws in this global era.

Chapter—30
Food Production

During the last 25 years, world agriculture successfully expanded food production faster than population growth. This can continue for the next 25 years and beyond, if appropriate action is taken. Although world food stocks are currently low and grain prices high, the world is not about to run out of food. We can produce enough food for future generations if we choose to do so.

The widespread food insecurity, unhealthy living conditions, and abject and absolute poverty in many developing countries are already threatening global stability. Failure to assure sustainable food security will foster the very conditions that will further destabilize and polarize the world in the years to come with tremendous consequences for all people.

The Basic Facts

Poverty is widespread in developing countries, with over 1.1 billion people living on a dollar a day or less per person. Human resource development in developing countries is lagging: 1 billion people lack access to health services, 1.3 billion do not have access to adequate sanitation systems, and one-third of primary school enrolls drop out by Grade 4. Natural resources, upon which future food production depends, are being degraded at alarming rates: almost 2 billion hectares of land have been degraded in the past 50 years: about 180 million hectares of forests have been converted to other uses during the 1980s, marine fisheries are collapsing around the world, and regional and seasonal water shortage afflict many developing countries. Improved appropriate technology is essential to increase productivity. Yet low-income food deficit developing countries are grossly underinvesting in agricultural research and many are reducing their support.

It calls for sustained action in **six** priority areas. **First,** we must selectively strengthen the capacity of developing country governments to perform appropriate functions such as establishing or clarifying property rights, promoting private-sector competition in agricultural markets, and maintaining appropriate macroeconomic environments. Predictability, transparency and continuity in policy making and enforcement must be pursued.

Investing in People

Second, we must invest more in poor people in order to enhance their productivity, health, and nutrition. It is not only unethical but economically wasteful that a large share of the world's population is malnourished, illiterate, sick, and without access to productive resources. Access to primary education, primary health care, reproductive care and family planning information, and clean water and sanitation must be assured for all people. Access by the poor to productive resources and remunerative employment must be improved. Empowerment of women must be supported.

Third, we must accelerate agricultural productivity. Agriculture is the life blood of the economy in low-income developing countries. In those countries, it provides up to three-quarters of all employment and half of all incomes. There are very strong links between agricultural productivity increases and broad-based economic growth in the rest of the economy. Agriculture is an engine of growth in low-income developing countries. National and international agricultural research systems must be mobilized to develop improved technologies focused on developing countries, and extension systems must be strengthened to disseminate the improved technologies and techniques. Low-income countries currently spend less than 0.5 per cent of the value of agricultural production on agricultural research compared to 2 per cent spent on agricultural research in middle and high-income countries. An increase of agricultural research expenditures in low-income countries to at least 1 per cent of the value of agricultural output is urgently needed, with a longer term target of 2 per cent. National agricultural research must be supported by a vibrant international agricultural research system that undertakes research with large international benefits applicable across boundaries. Current investments in international agricultural research are grossly inadequate to provide the support needed by developing countries. It is of critical importance that agricultural research result in reduced unit-costs of production. Such cost reductions will make food economically accessible to low-income consumers, and permit producer incomes to increase. To assure relevance of research and appropriate distribution of responsibilities, interactions between public sector agricultural research systems, farmers, private enterprises, and NGOs must be strengthened.

Fourth, we must assure sustainability in agricultural production and sound management of natural resources. Farmers, local communities, and governments must be encouraged to establish and enforce systems of rights to use and manage natural resources, to improve the way water is allocated and used, to reverse land degradation where it has occurred, to reduce the use of chemical pesticides and promote integrated pest management programmes, and to implement integrated soil fertility programmes in areas with low soil fertility. Local control over natural resources must be strengthened and local capacity for organisation and management improved. Investments in less-favoured geographical areas, that is, areas with agricultural potential, irregular rainfall patterns, and fragile soils must be expanded. Most poor people in developing countries reside in rural areas, and most rural poor reside in less-favoured areas. Yet, most investments, including agricultural research investments, still focus on the more-favoured areas. If we are serious about reducing poverty and protecting the natural resource base, the balance between the less-favoured and more-favoured areas must be redressed.

Fifth, we must reduce food marketing costs in low-income developing countries. The cost of bringing food from the producer to the consumer is very high in many of these countries. Efficient, effective, and low-cost agricultural markets must be developed in order to bring these costs down. Inefficient state-run firms in agricultural in-put markets must be phased out;

investment in developing and maintaining infrastructure, especially in rural areas, must be forthcoming; policies and institutions that favour large-scale, capital-intensive market agents over small-scale, labour-intensive ones must be removed; development of small-scale credit and savings institutions must be facilitated; and technical assistance to create or strengthen small-scale, labour-intensive competitive rural enterprises must be provided.

Sixth, we must expand and realign international development assistance. Many years ago, industrialized countries had agreed to allocate at least 0.7 per cent of the gross national product (GNP) to international assistance. Most countries have not reached or do not maintain this target. Not only must the industrialized countries increase international development assistance to reach the 0.7 per cent target, but they must realign it to low-income developing countries. Also, contrary to the middle- and higher-income developing countries, the poorest countries are not able to gain access to capital from the rapidly expanding international commercial capital market. Developing countries in turn must seek measures to diversify sources of external funding, stem capital flight; and improve the effectiveness of the aid they receive.

Chapter—31

Democracy and the Market Economy

Today the idea of democracy is triumphant; the model is in principle embraced in most countries the world over. You may say that the very word democracy has been hailed and misused earlier in history. The most repressing and totalitarian regimes have tried to mask themselves as "real" or "peoples" democracies. What has happened, however, is a historical demasking of these false pretences.

What exactly do we mean by democracy? There is now a general agreement that democracy cannot be defined by purpose or policy or levels of mass mobilisation. It must be defined as a political system where different parties or individuals compete for power through regular free elections where all adult citizens have a vote. Moreover, a democracy must uphold certain basic human rights and well-defined freedoms which make the political process possible, and respect the opinion and integrity of the individual. No other definitions hold, and we should be careful when we talk about "real" democracy versus "formal" democracy. A society which in real life upholds the constitutional or formal democratic principles and which in practice applies the rights these principles imply, is by definition a democracy. A society with a beautiful-sounding constitution but where none or few of these rights are respected is certainly not a democracy.

Democratic Government no Guarantee for Equality

It is important to understand that democratic government does not necessarily mean good government in the sense that those in power make wise or well-considered decisions. Nor does it mean that conflicts inherent in the society are reduced to a minimum. Demands for democracy, social justice and a better life have historically gone hand in hand, but this does not mean that the establishment of a democratic system actually does lead to an improvement in social conditions or equality. It is also quite clear that some societies have a sort of outer shell of democracy but in reality, exclude large groups of people from having any political influence whatsoever. The actual differences in living conditions are so enormous and so entrenched that these people have no confidence at all in the political system even if it is democratic according to the definition. In these cases—example in some Latin American countries—one can talk of a "masked hegemony with competing elites" where the outcome of struggles for power has little relevance for the masses. It is a sort of social and political half-authoritarian system—but disguised as a democracy—where the military often have a significant influence.

In the rhetoric of the day the terms market economy and democracy are used as if they were synonymous or at least naturally emerging at the same time. But this is wrong—or atleast misleading. When the market economy or capitalism finally established itself in the 1800s and came to characterize modern industrial civilisation, democracy was at best in its infancy. In fact one could argue that democracy grew out of the contradictions and social dynamism inherent in the market economy of the capitalistic system. In this century we have a long list of terrifying and repressive regimes which nevertheless upheld the virtues of a market economy. That some of these regimes have for ideological and security reasons been hailed as bastions against communism, and also dignified members of the so-called free world does not transform them into democracies. In this company it is perhaps unnecessary to remind ourselves that the colonial system was assuredly not democratic, but was certainly based on capitalistic or market economic principles. It is the sad but irrefutable historical coupling between Western democracy, colonialism, and the plundering of resources in the name of the market economy which for understandable reasons meant that many of the leaders of national liberation movements looked for other models for the development of their young nations. In this connection it can be worth remembering what Nelson Mandela said soon after his release from 26 years of prison in the market economic but racist state of South Africa.

"When we in ANC during 40 years struggled for democracy we were put in prison by the same people who are now telling us how we should behave to promote the democracy we have been rejected by all these years".

While we can see that a market economy does not automatically lead to democracy, a functioning democracy—as we have defined it—does seem to require some form of free economic system.

Democracy and Economic Freedom

Theoretically, it is conceivable that a political democracy could be combined with an economy totally controlled by the government—but experience has shown this to be very difficult. One could even argue that it is by definition impossible since democracy implies a certain freedom of economic choice and independent economic actors. A functioning democratic system presupposes what is now often referred to as a civil society—in practice, independent institutions, companies, organisations, the media etc., regulated by law but not subject to or controlled by those in power.

We must also see clearly that there are no unambiguous relations between economic growth, development and democracy. Democratic governments are neither very successful when it comes to structural reforms which may be to the disadvantage of important interests in the society, nor when it comes to welfare. The developing countries which have achieved the greatest success economically and socially over the last 20 years are the East Asian countries—which all have had various kinds of more are less authoritarian systems.

However, that does not mean that you can use these countries as models for the rest of the world. There is no globally valid link between an authoritarian form of regime and economic development, not even when development is defined only in terms of autocentric growth. Many social scientists—have tried to find some systematic connection between what we call development or modernisation on the one hand, and the political system on the other—but all have failed.

It is also obvious that one of several prerequisites for economic growth and development is legitimate and reasonably well functioning government and governance. If the free market is to be a motor for development and improved welfare, and not just a meeting place for robber barons, the mafia and speculators, you must have a regulating and supportive state. If economic history teaches us anything, it is just this. Consider the astounding development in Germany after the war, or in Japan and the other East Asian countries some years later. There are many differences, but what they have in common is a well-functioning government apparatus with a long tradition.

Today we find ourselves in a historical situation where a large number of countries in the former communist states of Europe, in Africa, Asia and Latin America are at one and the same time trying to establish a new democratic system and new economic mechanisms. The situation is unique, and the intrinsic problems are unprecedented. Democracy as an idea has triumphed but in its practice it is in profound trouble. It is no exaggeration to talk of the crisis of democracy.

The former communist countries are certainly in crisis. As a by-product of the past regimes, there is an intensive suspicion of the political institutions, of the state and the parties—and in this way also the legitimacy of democracy and the ability of the politicians to deal with the fundamental problems of society has been undermined. The lack of a democratic tradition is not overcome from one day to the next.

Many of the developing countries have similar difficulties. The introduction of a multiparty system does not in itself mean that one can manage the conflicts and social problems in a democratic way.

Countries in Transition

Both in the East and the South countries are trying, at one and the same time, to change the political and economic system. When the whole society is convulsed by economic changes, and where peoples' living conditions fundamentally change, it is not easy to develop and maintain a political system based on compromise and respect, including respect for minorities.

As in previous history the deep crises of legitimacy and general frustration feed national and ethnical conflicts. These conflicts establish themselves in societies where the authoritarian system, economic crises and the break down of traditional values rob people of any kind of kinship other than ethnical.

We cannot avoid seeing disturbing signs of this crisis of democracy also in the so-called "established democracies" of the rich countries.

It is obvious that the state of democracy varies from country to country, as do the reasons for a feeling of dejection. But there are some similarities too.

The continuing and noticeable internationalisation limits the national freedom of political choice, available alternatives, and makes it more difficult for people to see the connection between "politics" and their actual living conditions. The governments are restrained by international economic events. The reaction of the stock exchange may be more important than that of the voters. The election results influence the stock exchange prices—but is it perhaps not also so that the stock exchanges, indirectly, also influence the election results? People feel themselves to be the victims of major economic changes, but no one seems to be responsible and they themselves feel they have little chance of influencing the outcome. The absence of clearly identifiable alternatives between the larger political parties provides opportunities for the populists and the extremists.

There is indeed reason to reflect on the lessons of the history of our turbulent and cruel century.

Priority for Growth

There is today much concern about the lack of resources for such urgent needs as the reconstruction of the East, a concerted attack on poverty and human development in the poorest countries, and environmental investments of all kinds. If the growth of world output returns to the levels of the 1980s, total output would growth by about one trillion dollars a year. There is infact, no other way to resolve the economic and political crises multiplying in the world community than to give priority to the restoration of growth.

We are certainly not at the end of history as someone has argued. We are rather at a dramatic turning point, as moment of many possibilities and many dangers. What we do now, for a few years ahead, may direct the future for several decades—like the dramatic and fateful years immediately after the second world war. All nations, all governments, have a responsibility. The rich world has a special responsibility, not just moral because of its enormous economic and political power.

Chapter—32

Rural Poverty in India and Development as a Policy Challenge

Poverty can be overcome, and that the poor can increase their income and production within an appropriate framework. Part of that framework is made up of a flow of resources and local-level institutional development, and there is considerable scope for improvement in both. However, the impact of investment and organization is strictly determined by the nature of the policy environment. While project and programmes can bring some relief to the rural poor, substantial change needs a strong policy commitment. While the poor can overcome poverty, they will not be able to until this becomes a major focus of national policy and action. In the main, this sort of commitment has not been made in the past—at the expense of both the poor and overall development in many areas.

The current state of India is highly contradictory. On the one hand, there is proclamation of a new order; on the other, increasing value is given to sectional and short-term national and group interests. With an overt concern with India's poor goes an equal weight given to concern with economic mechanisms and relations that pay little attention to poverty and foster more inequality. The dangers of this situation are real. The lack of concrete attention being given to change will mean greater economic polarization. Greater polarization among the better-off, and between the better-off and the poor—means instability and a lack of consensus, a lack of legitimacy.

Poverty is far reaching, and ought to be curtailed. In a period in which resources everywhere appear restricted, this seems not to be an attractive proposition at the practical level. Welfare is everywhere giving way to production as an imperative, just as public expenditure is giving way to private accumulation. Poverty alleviation does not appear to be an idea whose time has come. The objections are great, but they are also misplaced. Poverty alleviation is not necessarily a drain upon accumulation, and it is not primarily a public activity. Poverty alleviation is primarily the activity of the poor themselves, and their progress necessarily involves productive expansion. If this potential for private expansion has not been realized, it is not because of the nature of the poor, it is because of the way in which national economic affairs have been organized. Economic policy has been oriented towards the better-off—not infrequently at the expense of the poor. Given the historic association between wealth and power, the definition of development in terms of the large and the wealthy is hardly surprising.

There is the possibility of associated growth involving both large-scale and small-scale production, the better-off and the poor. The realization of this possibility might result from a new social compact. This social compact is not a commitment to social safety nets and welfare, both of which seem to presuppose that the poor are somehow necessarily out of the growth field. It is a commitment to abolishing artificial and onerous terms of exchange that discriminate against the poor, to investing resources where there are real opportunities for gain, irrespective of whether the economic agents concerned are rich or poor, and to creating the space for the poor to organize to pursue their social and economic interests.

There is a need for a new growth model consistent with new social realities. While the 1980s was a period of clearing away many of the obstacles to development, it was not a period in which there emerged a clear vision of what represented the positive basis for growth, beyond, that is, a general prescription of market-driven operations. The model must pass from admonition to positive prescription to fuel growth by integrating the poor in their rightful place in the production function. It must redefine the position of public expenditure in the development process, and seek to establish market structures which are both equitable and open to the participation of the economically weaker elements of the population. Most of all it must revalue the position and contribution of the poor and small-scale producers in the growth process, particularly in the agricultural sector, but not exclusively agriculture.

This means that the issue is not so much one of less government, but of government, both national and local, finding a new rationale for action, including, *inter alia,* creating conditions that will effectively unleash the productive potential of the rural poor.

Financial flows to the poorest Indians are not likely to undergo a very major expansion, especially through private channels. Development will rely very much on the mobilization of their own resources, and many of these resources are in the hands of the poor, are indeed not only the human capital embodied in the poor but also their assets which, while small, individually are cumulatively important in India. The growth model for the 1990s will have to embrace that fact, and build upon it. The paradox of most development models is that they have emphasized the value of what Indians do not have while devaluing what they have: capital intensity has been promoted in situations of scarcity of capital, at the expense of abundant labour and of low-cost methods of manifold increase of the productivity of assets of which the poor do dispose. In a not very indirect way, the creation of poverty has been subsidized. Poverty alleviation is neither a special topic nor a low-cost substitute for growth. It is neither more nor less "social" than development in general. It is part of the formulation of any sustainable strategy of economic development. In the 1990s it may, and perhaps should, become the dominant issue—not as an alternative to the structural reorganizations of the 1980s, but as a means of filling a growth framework with substance.

Chapter—33
Lightening the Load for Women

Not only do women in India suffer greater poverty than men, they often have little choice but to pass it on to the next generation. Investing in women, therefore, is an effective way of building a better economic future for the poor.

Research findings from all sources are confirming what development practitioners have long observed: women are generally worse off economically than men, and the consequences of their poverty are more serious for future generations.

Women's poverty differs from that of men both in degree and in kind: women experience greater poverty and transmit their disadvantage more readily to their children, thus perpetuating the poverty cycle. At the same time, however, they are better able than men to protect children from the consequences of poverty.

It is this close connection between women's and children's fortunes that makes women's poverty a prime target for enlightened development practice. Anti-property policies need to reach poor women both to maximize social return on development investments and minimize the poverty of this and the next generation.

Breaking the Poverty Cycle

Poor women's rising participation in the world of paid work, however, does not necessarily guarantee a destiny of poverty. On the contrary, their earnings can protect children from poverty. Until fairly recently, the prevailing assumption was that any positive income effect of women's employment on children's health and well-being would be offset by negative effects of reduced child care time by working mothers or by the substitution of older siblings in child care. Recent studies, however, indicate a positive effect of women's employment on child health and nutrition. Women prefer to invest meagre earnings on child well-being and underscore the point that the income poor women earn can yield higher social benefits than income earned by men.

These positive effects of poor women's income-earning activities are not necessarily contradictory with the negative effects of women's increased work on their daughter's educational opportunities. It is likely that women need a minimum level of income to act on their preference to invest scarce resources on child well-being, below which their additional work perpetuates rather than halts poverty.

Policy and Research Implications

It is therefore desirable to implement policies that reinforce the virtuous cycle between women's and children's well-being that can occur in poor families when women have more income, and avoid those that can instead trigger a vicious cycle of deprivation between mothers and children. Circumstances which increase poor women's unpaid or very low-paid work can foster the perpetuation of disadvantage. These include the effects of declining household incomes during economic downturns, the decrease in service provision by the State which accompanies Structural adjustment programmes, and many community and child-centered interventions that rely heavily on women's unpaid time. Anti-poverty packages need to reinforce poor women's roles as economic producers and avoid actions which increase women's unpaid labour for the promotion of family child welfare.

Projects which increase women's productivity in home and market production and expand their employment options can help to turn the vicious cycle of poverty into a virtuous one. This necessitates executing agencies which can work with women, and budget allocations to strengthen the capacity of institutions to implement and monitor gender-responsive employment programmes for the poor.

The reach of project interventions is restricted, however. Their impact is often short-lived and while they can help to contain the cycle of poverty between mothers and children, they cannot in themselves transform women's economic activities. Changes in the policy environment are required for the latter. These include agricultural policies which target poor farmers and give women farmers access to land, credit and technical assistance; financial policies which promote the growth of small enterprises and foster entrepreneurship among women; and labour-intensive "pro-poor" economic growth policies. In addition, governments need to invest in upgrading women's occupational skills, and in a series of complementary measures, including overhauling social security systems, establishing gender friendly regulatory frameworks for agricultural and industrial growth, and legislate on child care options.

To guide these policies, we need: research that distinguishes families from households and seeks to understand the formation, structure and dynamics of families headed by women; longitudinal studies which provide a narrative for events in women's lives and assess the transmission of disadvantage between mothers and children; trend data which tracks changes in women's work as a result of changes in economic conditions and in implementation of economic and social policies; and analyses of the mechanics, costs and consequences of targeting interventions to female heads of households and poor women.

The policy-oriented research agenda is perhaps as ambitious as the policy agenda and both require funding. Investing in women should be an effective use of scarce development resources if these actions are guided by the basic principle of seeing women in India for what they are: economic and social agents and not merely passive recipients of welfare.

Chapter—34
Food First

By the time this day is over, about 40,000 human beings mostly children—will have died from hunger, malnutrition and related causes. Today and every day the deaths will mount, reaching an annual toll of 13 to 18 million. Few of these people will have been caught up in famine or other emergencies. Most will have suffered from a "silent" assault—the kind that seldom makes the headlines, but which claims its victims just as relentlessly.

It is intolerable that such deprivation and suffering should be allowed to exist in a world of potential food plenty. Having enough food is fundamental to all else. At the most basic level, this may entail humanitarian relief to assist people in emergency situations. In the transition from relief to development, however, we must look at systems for ensuring that societies have the capacity to produce or purchase the food they need and that it is accessible to all.

Sustainable food security fuses the goals of household food security and sustainable agriculture; it requires both. It requires looking not only at the aggregate supply of food, but also at the distribution of income and land, and at other issues: Do people have enough income to buy food? Enough land to grow their own food? Does the food distribution system deliver food where it is needed? How much food is wasted due to inadequate distribution systems? What are the implications of trends in population growth for future food needs? What is the status of women in society, and what opportunities do women have to alter rapid population growth rates? What is being done to regenerate the resource base for food production? These questions need to be asked and answered in every country.

The challenge of sustainable food security is immense, and it is growing. One billion people—20 per cent of the global population—are too poor to obtain enough food to sustain normal work. Half a billion are too poor to obtain the food needed for healthy growth of children and minimal activity of adults. Today's failure to feed people, however, may be but a prologue to a much larger failure in the future. Given likely population increases, world food output must triple over the next 50 years if the world's people are to have a nutritionally adequate diet. It will be difficult enough to achieve this expansion under favourable circumstances, and conditions may be far from favourable.

For example, according to recent estimates an area of about 1.2 billion hectares—the size of China and India combined—has experienced moderate to extreme soil deterioration since World War II as a result of human activities. Over three-fourths of that deterioration has occurred in the developing regions from causes such as overgrazing, deforestation, land clearing, unsound agricultural practices and increased soil salinity and water-logging, largely from irrigation. Other environmental threats to the agricultural resource base include loss of water and genetic resources, adverse effects of pesticides and climate change, both local and global.

At the most aggregate level, the required increase in food production could be met if production grew at the historic average, that is, at two per cent per annum rate achieved over the past half-century. But is this realistic? To produce three times more calories, all the land currently under cultivation around the world would, within 50 years, have to attain levels of productivity as high as those exhibited by the very best cropland today.

To this challenge add the possibility of diminished returns from the technological, energy and other inputs that have made agriculture so successful. Some experts believe that most of the potential for increased output of cereals—from improved plant varieties, from increased use of pesticides and fertilizers and from expanding the area under irrigation—has already been captured.

Viewed from this perspective, the goal of achieving sustainable food security in the decades ahead emerges as one of the greatest challenges humanity has ever faced. Agricultural output must be tripled, and people must have the income to buy the food they need. The erosion of the resource base must be halted and then reversed. Failure on any of these fronts will yield unprecedented human suffering.

What will it take to achieve sustainable food security? Obviously, the effort will have to be immense, both in size and complexity. Outlined below are a few simple (but no easy) steps that are absolutely essential elements of serious effort.

First, as citizens of the world, we must all come to see sustainable food security as a fundamental aspect of global peace and human security. This goes well beyond merely denouncing the use of food as a weapon.

Second, we must adopt concrete international goals, such as reducing world hunger by half over the next 10 years. We will never achieve the goal of sustainable food security unless we aim at specific milestones, and assess rigorously our progress in moving toward them.

Third, we must forge a true global partnership, a compact for sustainable food security. All countries—rich and poor—have important roles and responsibilities. There must be reciprocal responsibilities among nations, not one-way transfers.

Fourth, we must see deterioration of the agricultural resource base—terrestrial, aquatic and climatic—for what it is: a major threat to development and a major source of economic loss. Farmers are the largest group of environmental decision-makers in the world. We must ensure that they have the means to make sustainable development a reality where it counts—in the fields and fisheries.

Fifth, we must empower the people who work the land and who keep it productive. They are in the best position to decide the most appropriate ways to graft new technology into their own traditional knowledge of seed selection, plant protection and nutrient-cycling. Special emphasis should be given to the role of women, the main providers for two-thirds of the poorest households in the developing world, as well as the producers of 60 per cent of all food grown and consumed locally.

Sixth, we must build the capacities of developing countries, both in government and in civil society. Capacity-building means empowerment for self-reliance. It means strengthening national capacities both inside and outside government. This is essential for recognition and analysis of problems, for decision-making on courses of action and for management of systems and processes.

Seventh, not only must we build capacity in developing countries, we must also create linkages among researchers in industrial and developing countries. This will help minimize the time lag between discovery and practical utilization. In addition, analysts from various countries must work together to examine future food security issues with different scenarios of population growth, agricultural productivity, markets and trade, climate change, loss of soil and bio-diversity and, last but not least, political instability, in order to devise options for rational choices.

We know a good deal about how to rid the world of the scourge of hunger, and how to begin to move toward sustainable food security on a global basis. We know that economic growth and prosperity are necessary though not sufficient, conditions for eradicating hunger. We also know that development efforts must encompass not only food production, but also socio-economic factors, including sustainable livelihoods for poor families, the implications of population growth rates, the status of women and girls and so forth. We also know that good words are not enough. Now more than ever before it is crucial that we marshal the political will to achieve our goals.

Chapter—35

Aid Effectiveness as a Multi-level Process

Parallel to the widerspread decrease of aid resources provided by donor countries to developing countries in recent years, debate and research on how to make aid more effective has become a major concern. Usually, it is suggested that decades of development assistance have at best produced marginal results in terms of improving development levels in the South. Little mention is made of donors' policy shortcomings and the negative impact of these on efforts aimed at reforming and redefining development cooperation in order to enhance aid effectiveness. The policy parameters and operating frameworks of existing aid policies continue to inhibit higher degrees of aid effectiveness. In many donor countries, opinion polls indicate waning public support for development aid.

Increasingly, the moral case for aid is called into question and deeper world market integration tends to be seen as the panacea to continued economic decline and social destabilisation in the South. Against this background, cooperation between donor and recipient actors is faced with a duel uphill struggle. First fewer resources can be mobilized to meet growing developmental needs. On the other hand, to organize and manage development policies and programmes in a result-oriented manner, grows more difficult. The threat of further aid cuts and of further drops of public support for providing aid become ever more real. A closer look at the organizational complexities and political constraints under which development cooperation is expected to perform effectively may help to improve current aid management approaches.

Towards Conceptual Clarity

At first sight, catchy definitions of what constitutes effective aid might appear attractive to use, in particular with regard to economic indicators, the term "aid effectiveness" is easily used in the same vein as "efficiency", "significance" of "impact" of aid. At times, obsession to measure and demonstrate the results of aid supported development processes ca be observed among policy-makers and administrators on the donor side. Still the understanding of aid and its effectiveness as being part and parcel of a cooperation relationship between donor and recipient side parties, is scarcely embedded in practice. To determine how to make aid more effective requires more than a quick impact analysis of an individual and perhaps even isolated development project. Consequently, defining the concept of aid effectiveness needs to take into account at what levels cooperation is focused on. To strive for sustainable and effective modes of development cooperation will entail the need to combine recipient ownership of the development process with donor accountability concerns.

Performance expectations cannot be exclusively placed on the recipient while donor interests, their aid management systems and procedures remain unchanged.

An extended and more analytical process oriented definition should take into account four main aspects of aid effectiveness:

(a) Effective aid must relate to the building and/or strengthening of in-country aid management capacity:

(b) To maximize the degree of aid effectiveness, local ownership of the aid process is essential: from setting of priorities through policy formulation and implementation on to the evaluation stages of the process;

(c) Increasing recipient side capabilities to take charge of aid relationship, will need to be combined with arrangements to meet legitimate donor accountability concerns;

(d) Aid effectiveness is a two-faceted objective; its realisation is equally dependent on increased

transparency of donor motives and on dropping of nondevelopmental, political and economic aid objectives of donors.

In addition a broader range of stakeholders in the aid relationship needs to be actively involved; extending beyond accountable government and implementing agencies, to include democratic institutions and organisations of civil society and of the private sector.

Applying any definition of aid effectiveness without disaggregating macro-economic data and taking into account country specificity will only lead to unhelpful generalisations about aid and its effectiveness. It would seem more appropriate to adopt working definitions against which to assess effectiveness of aid resources at a country-specific level. On such a basis one could expect to arrive at more reliable indicators of how well aid resources contribute to improving developmental standards and meeting exiting needs.

From Definition to Success-Key Requirements

Having reached agreement between the recipient and donor on what should constitute effectiveness of aid is only a starting point. Embarking on democratic, peaceful and participatory patterns of economic and social development must follow: to arrive at significant and lasting improvement in many of the least developed countries will be a long-term process. This being said, it is crucial to design and implement such forms of development cooperation which involve a wide range of recipient side actors, not only from the government side but also from civil society at large. Seen as a process of increasing inclusion of intended beneficiaries of aid, the commitment to decentralize as well as entrust aid and its management grows in importance.

To fully capture Third World development realities, policy frameworks inspired by neoliberalist-type of development concepts and theories are grossly inadequate. The views and positions on aid articulated in the World Bank and the IMF, or in many if not most bilateral aid administrations in OECD countries, represent only one side of today's international cooperation, namely the donor side. The major weakness to point out with respect to this locus of debate, is a profound under-representation if not even a total absence of recipient experiences and perceptions on aid in general and on its effectiveness in particular. There should be little doubt that ignoring to not actively identifying and involving such perceptions, leads to strongly donor driven aid.

To circumvent recipient side insights and views on strengths and weaknesses of aid strategies and mechanisms, will result in limited local commitment and sense of ownership over the aid process. Mutual decision-making between donors and recipients remains a rare policy approach. Aid procedures that are based on local management and less control-oriented donor roles in the aid process are still exceptions in development cooperation.

Structurally, in terms of the policy environment within which development aid is expected to function, the overriding policy framework is general based on structural adjustment policies (SAP). But the underlying conclusion made by proponents of SAPs that these policies induce aid effectiveness, has yet to be proven valid. It must suffice at this point to emphasize that there is no a priori relationship between world market integration under structural adjustment and sustainable development in poor countries. Aid to these countries which is solely intended to reinforce fundamentally uneven and unequal patterns of world market integration should be scrutinized critically.

Some central issues need to be addressed in the course of improving aid and its effectiveness:

- institutional dimensions of aid relationships require strong policy-attention, both on the donor and the receipt side;
- capacities to effectively identify and formulate aid priorities need to be strengthened in recipient countries;
- local capacities to sustain reform efforts must be reinforced.

Levels of Intervention

If the design of aid and the terms upon which it is provided to a developing country are largely determined by the donor, the aid relationship can be characterised as essentially hierarchical. Recipient side views will rarely surface, as they are either not identified or not well formulated. Possibilities of a recipient-led development strategies can be limited. Unless scope is provided to the recipient side actors to assume responsibilities, aid effectiveness is likely to remain low of fluctuating, and the sustainability of donor aid efforts will remain doubtful.

National planning processes and courses of national development in recipient countries should be seen as most effective where they are led under local responsibility and control. To arrive at this ideal situation, gaps need to be reduced and closed at the various intervention levels.

Donor aid resources provide valuable support for this process. Their effectiveness in meeting long-term objective of aid will need to be assessed on the basis of how well they perform at the different levels. Individual donors will expectedly perform differently at the various levels. What will prove to be the ultimate test for effectiveness is how well the donor aid performance accomplishes the broader objectives of development cooperation and how well it includes sustainable results.

In the analytical frameworks outlined here, development cooperation would seem to be confronted with the effectiveness gaps at the.

- structural level: International trade and investment patterns, debt problems and world market integration process appear as long-term constraining factors upon aid and its effectiveness;
- at the policy level, dialogue and partnership in development cooperation are instrumental factors in recluding planning and coordination gaps with regard to policy analysis and formulation;
- the institutional level is where pertinent capacity gaps exist: capacity development efforts of donor and

technical assistance measures play an important role in addressing weaknesses in aid effectiveness within a country's institutional setting;

- finally, at the level of aid projects (programmes), it is generally the lack of sustainability of aid interventions which cause development activities to falter once donor support decreases or stops. In addition to technical cooperation, financial and material inputs serve to maintain project momentum and goal realisation: the issue of how to develop local capacity sufficiently in order for indigenous organisations to continue project activities initially supported by donor aid, remains the most important issue to address at this level.

Fostering Aid Effectiveness

Donor and recipient development efforts are too often isolated from one another, or poorly co-ordinated. They fail to address managerial and implementation bottlenecks. Cross-sectorial linkages, as well as interdisciplinary approaches to aid problems are only slowly gaining ground. It is increasingly obvious that decisions on aid issues are subjected to concerns outside of the responsible ministry: finance ministers, and unfortunately even defense ministers have a strong say in how much aid is to be provided, where it is to be concentrated and under what terms to be utilised. Inside of recipient countries, large portions of national budgets are allocated to non-development priorities with little or no impact on alleviating urgent poverty problems.

Development cooperation may make the biggest impact and be executed most effectively where donors and recipients agree upon multi-level aid strategies. To give an example: building a road to a remote rural area may well be done in an effective project manner; it is equally important to have a functioning transport authority in place to ensure maintenance of the roads. If this authority operates within nationally defined infrastructure policy, best in accord with national trade and investment priorities, then the effectiveness of the project-level road building programme has a good chance of being high.

Institutional changes to set the stage for a profound reform process in development cooperation are needed. Reprioritising national budgets to reflect identified in country development need may be one step. Setting up policy evaluation and formulation units can be complimentary measures. Deregulating markets and investment rules may serve to please donors, but dumping of cheap products which strangle local production efforts may easily result. Regional cooperation, including intensified South-South cooperation can provide some counterbalance. There are only a few areas where changes in the current system of development cooperation can occur, with a view to better manage the complexities of aid and the social, cultural, economic and political backgrounds against which they take place. The will and commitment to take policy action in both donor and recipient countries, through the broadest range of stakeholders and institutions as possible, will be the test for genuine efforts at improving development relations between North and South and organising cooperation effectively.

Chapter—36

Income Gap Widens

The gap in income among the people of the world has been widening. In 1960, according to United Nations statisticians, the richest 20 per cent of the world's people received 30 times more income than the poorest 20 per cent. By 1991, they were getting 61 times more. While the poorest one-fifth in 1960 received a meager 2.3 per cent of world income, by 1991 that revenue share had fallen to 1.4 per cent. The income share of the richest fifth, meanwhile, rose from 70 per cent to 85 per cent.

These disparities prevail both among countries and within them, and the large gap between individuals world wide reflects the combination of both of those splits. Almost four-fifths of all people live in the developing world, where incomes are only fraction of those in industrial countries. In turn, within countries in both categories, gaps in income between citizens can be even wider.

The widest income gap reported within a country is in Botswana, where during the 1980s the richest 20 per cent of society received over 47 times more income than the poorest 20 per cent. Brazil was second, with a ratio of 32 to 1. In Guatemala and Panama, the ratio stood at 30 to 1.

The rapidly growing economies of East Asia have had income patterns similar to those of Western Europe and North America, with the richest one-fifth often earning 5 to 10 times more than the poorest fifth. In South Asia, India, Bangladesh, and Pakistan have had relatively even distributions on income with the richest 20 per cent getting only four to five times more than the poorest quintile. Some countries that have had military conflicts apparently based in part on inequities among citizens, nevertheless have relatively even income distributions.

The split between countries and people can be seen in the marketplace. The value of luxury good sales world-wide—high-fashion clothing and top-of-the-line autos, for example-exceeds the gross national products of two-thirds of the world's countries. The world's average income, roughly $4,000 a year, is well below the U.S poverty line.

The poorest fifth of the world accounted for 0.9 per cent of world trade, 1.1 per cent of global domestic investment, 0.9 per cent of global domestic savings, and just 0.2 per cent of global commercial credit at the beginning of the 1990s. Each of those shares declined between 1960 and 1990.

These disparities are reflected in the consumption of many resources. At the start of this decade, industrial countries home to roughly a fifth of the world's population, accounted for about 86 per cent of the consumption of aluminium, and chemicals, 81 per cent of the paper, 80 per cent of the iron and steel, and three-quarters of the timber and energy. Since then, economic growth in developing countries has probably reduced these percentages. China's ecohomy, for example, is more than 50 per cent larger now than it was in 1990, and developing countries have passed industrial ones in fertilizer consumption.

Uneven income distribution is shaping some of the most important trends in the world today. It raises crime rates, for example. And it drives migration. People have long responded to economic disparities by following a path from poor regions to richer ones, as tens of millions of workers chase higher wages and better opportunities. Some 1.6 million Asians and Middle Easterners were working in Kuwait and Saudi Arabia before they fled war in 1991, and at least 2.5 million Mexicans live in the United States.

The same is true within countries: rising disparities of income are adding to the growth of cities thorough rural-to-urban migration. Latin America, with some of the highest disparities of income among its citizens, is also the most urbanized region of the developing world—not entirely by coincidence. Since 1950, city dwellers there have risen from 42 per cent of the population to 73 per cent.

For many years, China had one of the most equal distributions of income in the world. But now that is changing, as incomes in its southern provinces and special economic zones soar while those in rural areas rise much more slowly. Also not coincidentally, the Chinese National Academy of Social Sciences forecasts that by 2010, half the population will live in cities, compared with 28 per cent today and only 10 per cent in the early 1980s.

In the early 1990s, developing world economies, especially in East Asia, have grown faster than the economies of the industrial countries. This has the potential to shrink disparities of income, if poorer countries continue to catch up. Yet even if the gaps among countries narrow, the gaps between people may not, because economic growth is distributed so unevently within nations. Despite the recent restoration of economic growth in Latin America, no progress is expected in reducing poverty, which is even likely to increase slightly.

Meanwhile, in some regions almost no one has been getting richer. The per capita income of most sub-Saharan African nations actually fell during the 1980's. In sub-Saharan Africa, the poorest geographic region, an estimated one-third of all a college graduates have left the continent. That loss of talented people, due in large part to poverty and a lack of opportunities in Africa, will make it even more difficult for the continent to advance.

The economic growth that has the potential to close income gaps among peoples in the developing world is instead becoming a splitting off, with some parts of societies joining the industrial world while others remain behind. Singapore, Hongkong, and Taiwan have begun to look like wealthy industrial countries, for example. Now parts of China are following, as are the wealthier segments of Latin American society and of Southeast Asian countries. This is good news for members of the middle-income countries and for the world. But it may do little to help the poorest fifth of humanity.

Chapter—37

Food for the Billions

Will there be enough food to feed 8 billion people who will live on earth in 25 years' time? Surprisingly few people, at least in the industrial countries, seem to be overly concerned with this question. Whereas the world conferences on the environment, on women, human rights or social issues which were held in recent years were preceded and accompanied by intensive public debate, food does not seem to be a burning issue. Don't we have mountains of surplus food, people ask. Do we not have to pay our farmers to leave their land idle in order not to add to the glut on the world markets? And hasn't the Green Revolution ended famine even in countries like India which used to be a synonym for hungry people? So where is the problem?

The advance made in agricultural production since beginning against a background of imminent crisis are indeed remarkable. In only 20 years, yields of major crops like rice, maize and wheat in developing countries went up by 80 per cent outpacing even the rapid increase in population. But this growth in yields has slowed down in recent years, and the aim of "food for all" is once again becoming elusive. About 800 million people still do not have access to enough food to meet their basic daily needs, nearly 200 million children suffer from protein and energy deficiencies, 88 countries—44 of them in Africa—have a deficit in food production.

Everyone wants to increase food security. The definition is that "food be available at all times, that all persons have means of access to it, that it be nutritionally adequate in terms of quantity, quality and variety, and that it be acceptable within the given culture". To achieve this goal, more food must be produced—much more, because we must not only adequately feed the 5.8 billion people already on earth, but also the additional two billion who will be added to world population in the next 25 years. Critics argue that the problem is not one of production alone, but one of poverty elimination. People are hungry not because there is no food, but because they have no money to buy it, these critics say. Available resources must be better distributed to end hunger in the world.

However, even if we succeed to eliminate poverty in the next few decades—a feat which appears highly unlikely—there would still be the need to boost production, because with rising incomes people also want to eat more and better food including meat. As can already be observed in the countries of East Asia, the newly acquired wealth leads to higher consumption levels which puts additional strains on available resources are getting scarcer. Agricultural lands are being degraded at alarming speed by erosion, salinity, desertification or disappear altogether due to urban or infrastructure development. It has been estimated that 40 per cent of productive land now has diminished capacity to supply benefits to humanity due to direct human impacts of land use. Water for agricultural purposes is getting scarcer almost everywhere, and there are hardly any land reserves to be brought into production to widen the agricultural base.

In this situation, there is no alternative to increasing and improving production from the existing land area. This can only be done through research which finds the best varieties which will bring the highest yields at the lowest cost to the environment. Sustainable agriculture is the key notion—one that maintains bio-diversity, uses as little chemical inputs as possible and does not overexploit water and soil resources.

In recent years, agricultural research has been neglected—partly because of the erroneous belief that with mountains of meat and lakes of milk further production increases were not desirable. Since global grain production has stagnated and world stocks have reached an alarmingly low last year, there has been a noticeable change of mind. To raise the awareness among governments around the world that promotion of agriculture is urgent if hunger is to be avoided in the next century.

Important work is already being done by the international agricultural research institutes which promoted the Green Revolution in the sixties and seventies and are now again in the forefront of finding solutions to the daunting task of feeding 8 billion people by the year 2020. The International Rice Research Institute (IRRI) in the Philippines, the Maize and Wheat Research Institute (CIMMYT) in Mexico or institutes like ICARDA in Syria and ICRISAT in India which work on agriculture in semi-arid and dry areas, are all seeking solutions to the problem of raising production while at the same time preserving the environment. These institutions as well as national agricultural research institutions need all the support from the public and, of course, appropriate funding, to help them accomplish their task.

The scientists are optimistic that they can develop the varieties and farming systems which will allow mankind to feed everyone on earth well into the next century. But the task is not for the scientists alone. An economic and political order must also be in place which makes it possible to eradicate poverty and allow everyone to enjoy the benefits that science can offer. Feeding the billions is, therefore not only a scientific, but first and foremost a political.

Chapter—38

NGOs—Better than the State

Non-governmental organizations have become the new hope of development cooperation. Criticism of official and multilateral development assistance is mounting. After more than four decades of international cooperation, there is more poverty in the Third World (with the exception of a few countries) than ever before. It has become clear that existing instruments cannot bring about change. Even the large donor organizations doubt their own ability to solve problems and find their doubts confirmed by internal evaluations. What led to this state of affairs, and is there reason to hope that the NGOs can do a better job?

Development assistance started in 1949 with U.S. President Harry Truman's famous Point Four Program (named after Point 4 of his inaugural speech in Congress on January 20, 1949) as a continuation of the Marshall Plan. The policy of containment of communism, which was originally restricted to Europe, thus became a global strategy. This origin was the reason that development assistance was geared from the beginning exclusively to governments, and not to social groups in the developing countries. The accusation that the U.S.A. as well as the other Western donors were willing to provide development assistance to any government, even the most under democratic and corrupt one, as long as was it an ally against communism, was never dropped.

Four decades later, when hardly anyone remembered the origins of this policy, the original goal was reached: Communism collapsed. In the interim, development assistance became independent: what was merely a means to an end for Truman in 1949 had became the goal itself: Liberation of all people not only from oppression, but also from hunger, want and desperation. However, it was now conceded, although hesitantly, that this particular goal had not been met: that in many countries a corrupt and dictatorial state class had been kept alive rather than development, and that democratization had in fact been obstructed.

Simultaneously, an intensive discussion of two new themes began in intellectual circles in the U.S. The return of ethics in politics, and a stronger influence of citizens in public affairs—against the background of governments which were no longer trusted to be able to solve social problems. Both themes have by now reached. Europe under the labels "Communitarianism" and "civil society" where they were taken up by the "new social movements". These included North-NGOs which are active in development cooporation and work with partner organizations in the south. It is important not to lose sight of this correlation with society's broader change of values.

The NGOs argue that they can circumvent the unwieldy bureaucratic planning and administration process; that they are flexible, efficient, close to the target groups, and democratic at the grassroots level, and that their funds flow directly to the poor. How accurate is this claim?

Little is known in the North about the NGOs of the South. The rural reconstruction movements, which exist in several Asian countries, date back to the twenties. Today, they are large organizations with hundreds of thousands of staff members. In India and Sri Lanka, groups try to realize the ideas of Mahatma Gandhi. In Africa, self-help and solidarity groups at the village level have been a tradition for centuries. Ethnologists used to characterize them as "secret societies". The large organizations, which were established in Africa (later than in Asia) a few years ago, build on this tradition. In Latin America, an attempt is made to revive the models of cooperative work in the pre-Columbian era.

It is a myth that these groups are egalitarian grassroots organizations. Those that actually function, at the village as well as at the regional or national level, do so, thanks to the selfless involvement of individual persons, who are able to motivate others, come up with ideas, cooordinate efforts, and bring about decisions. Social science has known since the studies of group dynamics and "democratic leadership" in the U.S. in the thirties that groups cannot be effective without such people. In the North they cannot work "directly with the poor" because this would presuppose that again we would be on location. The assistance depends on the cooperation of local organizations, which means their leaders. We tend to forget this too easily in our development jargon. The real chance for NGO leaders lies in the fact that they do not have to prevail against a rigid, bureaucratic apparatus which tries to stop novel ideas just because they are new. On the other hand, this constellation also harbours the danger that imperiousness and autocratic structures will expand within the NGO sector just as at the state level. Who actually monitors the NGOs? Not just government ministers have been known to build their own private residences with development aid money. Some NGO executives are already guilty of doing the same.

Chapter—39

Poverty in India

"It is morning in a remote farming area in India. As her husband harnesses a bullock to plough their field, a woman pounds the grain she will use for the day's main meal. Three kilometres away, their children are collecting fuel wood and water before starting their morning walk to school".

"After school, they help their mother light a fire with a few sticks, milk the cow and collect the sundried grain. That evening, as the family rests around the hearth, father worries about how to sell his onions before they spoil and the price falls. Before sleeping his wife prepares a basket of home-grown vegetables to sell next day at the village market five kilometres away. With the taking, she hopes to buy a kerosene lamp although she might not have enough cash left to buy the kerosene immediately..."

That description of rural life is a daily reality for hundreds of millions of families throughout India. Rural poverty, 1990s means subsistence on the meagre earnings of wage labour or unreliable harvests from small plots of land. It means raising a family without safe drinking water or proper sanitation, suffering disease or injury without medical assistance. In times of unemployment or crop failure, it means living with the pangs of hunger—and the risk of death by famine.

Inside the Poverty Trap

Poverty in rural India is created and perpetuated by a number of closely interlinked socio-economic processes.

1. Policies and institutional arrangements biased against the poor exclude them from the benefits of

development, frustrate their productive potential and accentuate the impact of other poverty processes. Institutional processes that perpetuate rural poverty include lack of access to land, inequitable sharecropping and tenancy arrangements, poor markets. limited access to credit, inputs and technology, and ineffective extension services. Other constraints are lack of training facilities, inadequate research related to smallholder farming systems, and last but not least a lack of grassroots institutions needed to foster people's participation.

Policy and institutional biases have short and long-term impacts. In the short term, the poor are unable to earn enough to meet nutritional requirements or to take advantage of the market. "In the longer term", "poor households continue to lag behind because they do not generate a surplus for investment, nor do they have access to investment opportunities. Moreover, the rural poor may be forced to overuse resources, which undermines productivity and income".

2. Even today dualistic agrarian structures originating in colonial times persist. In India, highly capitalized large and medium-sized farms have virtually monopolistic control over land and labour at the expense of the small farm sector. Large scale commercial producers control the best farm land. Resources have been funelled into irrigated plantations producing cotton and mechanized cultivation of sorghum. In marginal areas, mechanization has led to environmental degradation and the loss of seasonal grazing and stock routes for pastoralists.

   "Thus, side by side with modern agriculture, millions of marginal farmers and herdsmen subsist far below the poverty line". This dualism severely limits their capacity to grow food and accumulate capital. They lack marketable surpluses, and incentives and opportunities to save and invest.

3. Rapid population growth can cause and perpetuate

rural poverty by increasing pressure on limited productive resources, social services and employment, as well as—paradoxically—creating labour shortages through outmigration.

The most obvious consequence of rapid population growth is that, even with relatively high rates of economic growth, improvements in living conditions are limited. Total saving in the economy declines, leaving fewer resources for investment in human development. Negative consequences are most acute in rural areas. Growing population often combined with traditional laws of inheritance—has led to fragmentation of holdings, degradation of crop and pasture land, and falling yields. In areas with unequal distribution of land, rapid population growth has accelerated proletarization of the rural work force and reduced incomes.

4. Rural poverty malnutrition and undernutrition are closely linked to environmental degradation. Poor people in marginal areas are destroying natural resources as they struggle to keep their production systems sustainable. In acute shortage of arable land has forced farmers to reduce the length of fallow periods and plough up land previously reserved for grazing. These practices have led to declining yields, soil depletion and further impoverishment. Population pressure is pushing weaker members of the rural community into ecologically vulnerable areas.

Degradation of the environment is strongly linked to house-hold food insecurity and lack of fuel. Much of the fragile forest cover has been destroyed by poor rural people in the search for grazing land and fuel wood.

Government policies have also wrought environmental damage. A rapid expansion of areas under crops often accelerates deforestation and land degradation. Programmes to expand cereal production into marginal areas, subsidized capital to support commercial operations subsidies for inappropriate technologies and excessive transfer of income out of the agricultural sector may undermine the sustainability of smallholders and pastoralists' production systems.

Inadequate public investment in off-farm employment and infrastructure, a lack of price incentives and inadequate access to modern agricultural inputs and services discourage investment in land conservation, leading to further overuse and degradation.

5. As poverty undermines traditional social bonds, the marginalization of women has become a fact of rural life in India. With little or no access to land, millions of women depend on casual employment on meagre wages. Often, they farm fragmented plots of poor quality. Limited access to inputs, extension, training and credit limits, in turn, their ability to enter commercial agriculture.

   The exodus of males in search of work in urban areas (itself an indicator of poverty) has serious consequences for the women they leave behind. Output from land often falls and less attention is paid to maintenance, setting the stage for a long-term decline in productivity. Many female headed households have abandoned the use of oxen for ploughing, some plough and plant late and others no longer weed their fields.

6. The ethnic or cultural marginalization of tribal or minority populations also plays a role in poverty. Many of these groups are further threatened by newly marginalized groups—as the expansion of cultivation reduces the grazing areas of nomadic herders.

7. Exploitative middlemen also perpetuate rural poverty. Landlords exploit share croppers and tenants, moneylenders exploit debtors, and traders exploit small scale producers. During seasonal food shortages, the poor may have to borrow money at interest rates exceeding 20 per cent a month. Forced to devote most

of their energies to debt servicing, they sink deeper into the poverty trap.

In some cases, government controlled cooperatives and government agencies whose task is to protect the poor may themselves practise forms of exploitation. Heavy levies imposed by government agencies have damaged small farmers. Large, inefficient bureaucracies are paid for by the productive sectors of the community and frequently contribute to the accumulation of large budget deficits.

8. Political troubles and civil strife have had a disastrous impact on the rural poor. One effect is the disruption of development assistance to the rural poor, both from national and international agencies. Another is the transformation of many producers into consumers of social services with serious consequences for production, savings, capital accumulation and investment.

9. The international economic environment directly influences the well-being of the Indian poor. Falling commodity prices and protectionist policies in India affect the employment and incomes of plantation workers and small-holders producing for export, particularly those relying heavily on a few agricultural commodities. Changes in international interest rates have repeatedly hurt small-scale producers in debt-burdened India, while world grain price increase has triggered rural famines.

The net flow of development resources to agriculture also affects rural poverty. Official development funding for food and agriculture increased between 1975 and 1982, but has fluctuated irregularly since. Moreover, concern with trade balances is diverting resources to export crops, sometimes at the expense of traditional crops grown by poor farmers.

Chapter—40

The Future of Work

The advent of an 'intangible' economy does not mean the end of work. But it does mean the end of familiar routines and rhythms, of job security, of rigid hierarchies and career planning.

People are worried about the far-reaching transformation of the economy. Are we heading for "the end of work". Yes, we have reached the end of the road. We are no longer creating jobs in industry and automation is sure to reduce their number in the services sector. The quantity of work is thus inexorably bound to decrease.

This thesis may be popular, but it is also mistaken and harmful. History shows that technological innovation has always created jobs on a large scale. In no way is the current trend leading to "the end of work". Just the opposite: the new economy contains huge pools of new jobs which can more than make up for the inevitable loss of traditional jobs.

Dematerialization—the shift away from material products-is revolutionizing all aspects of work—its nature, its organization and its relationship with other activities. Its function is no longer just the manufacture of physical objects but the handling of data, images and symbols. The content of jobs is becoming more abstract. Skilled workers need to know a lot more about mathematics than their fathers or grandfathers did. Even milking cows and manufacturing require more and more calculation, evaluation and control.

Financial Markets that Never Sleep

The organization as well as the product of work is also becoming increasingly intangible. The unity of time, space and action which characterized work in the industrial economy has disintegrated. Work is no longer a regular eight-hours-a-day, five-days-a-week routine. New rhythms have appeared—the hectic pace of financial markets which never sleep, the ups-and-downs of life in show business and the uncertainties of "just-in-time" production where components are delivered a few moments before the final product is assembled.

The new jobs are quitting familiar workplaces such as factories, offices and warehouses. Telework is increasing. Europe's teleworkers may number 10 million by the year 2000, up from one million in 1994.

This upheaval of worktime and workspace is going hand in hand with a functional explosion. The range of skills and types of work is expanding all the time. In the United States, the number of job categories has risen from eighty in the 1940s to nearly 800 today. At the same time, trades are dying out faster and faster, especially in information technology where many jobs have a short life of only a few years. Jobs are becoming simultaneously more evanescent and more pervasive, more dissociated and more integrated. On the one hand, fragmentation in time and space seems to be more extensive than it was in the industrial economy. On the other, information technology is strengthening the links between stages of work and creating an overall fluidity.

Disparities in Productivity

The new forms of work are non-linear. When handling information, knowledge and feelings, there is no direct relationship between the amount of efforts and the final result. This makes for very wide disparities in productivity. In industry, the ratio of the performance of an average worker to that of a good one is no more than one to five. But in immaterial work, an excellent programmer can be a hundred times more productive than an average one.

Non-linear work means non-linear organization. The notion of a rigid, formal hierarchy based on unchanging criteria no longer makes much sense. All that matters now is technical, scientific or artistic skill and the ability to establish a solid relationship with the customer. Functional hierarchy is replaced by "brainpower"- -authority gravitates to those who create and control the new stock of intangible assets: data, brand image, technological know-how and human capital.

The new techniques for managing human resources are individualizing the assessment of performance. Two people doing the same job may have different salaries and different status. Automatic across-the-board pay rises are being dropped and replaced by bonuses linked to results. There are no sinecures in the new business enterprise, either for rank-and-file employees, supervisors or technicians—the supposed beneficiaries of the new knowledge economy.

Business leaders are no longer a protected species. The head of a big American firm is ten times more likely to be sacked for poor performance now than was the case twenty years ago. The notions of loyalty and of indissoluble links between a firm and its employees are losing their meaning.

The changing nature of work has led to a big increase in so-called non-typical jobs, including part-time, temporary and flexi-time work and short-term contracts. Almost all the jobs created in Europe between 1992 and 1996 were part-time. This trend worries many observers who see it as hidden under-employment or disguised unemployment. But they are overly pessimistic. The growth of non-typical jobs is the result of the Convergence of several persistent developments.

Where the New Jobs Are

The shrinking number of jobs in traditional sectors of the economy seems to be a general and irreversible trend. In rich countries as a whole, the share of industrial jobs fell from 28 per cent in 1970 to 18 per cent in 1994. Meanwhile, the share of the services sector grew steadily. Four major new sources of jobs can be identified.

Handling information and knowledge: Computer services, research and development, teaching and training account for 40 per cent of knowledge workers. These high-intensity knowledge activities comprised 43 per cent of all new jobs created in the United States between 1990 and 1995, but only 28 per cent of total jobs.

Information technology: Here there is a shortage of personnel. Professional groups are sounding the alarm and calling on governments to help. In the European Union countries, the imbalance between supply and demand is such that half a million jobs are waiting to be filled.

The health sector: The growth of high-intensity knowledge services in this field is related to increased life expectancy and the ageing of the population, and the demand for physical and psychological well-being is also steadily increasing. The growth of expenditure on health is persistent and widespread. For the OECD countries as a whole, this spending grew from 3.9 per cent of GDP in 1960 to 7.2 per cent in 1980 and 8.4 per cent in 1992.

The leisure economy: This has triggered the expansion of cultural, sporting and leisure services. It ranges from amusement parks and rock concerts to cultural events such as opera and major art exhibitions. The products of the culture industries have become mass consumer items. Never before have people read so much, listened to so much classical music or visited so many museums. Information technology is also going to add to this vast range of consumer choice. In southern California and New York, the entertainment and multimedia professions are among the main sources of new jobs.

In the labour market, the increase in non-typical jobs is one of the ways in which employers are responding to the pressures of competition and adapting to a global economy which functions seven days a week, twenty-four hours a day. To cope with the new situation, firms are having to figure out how they can use their workers more efficiently and flexibly.

The growth of non-traditional jobs is also due to changing demand. Consumers want to be able to buy a very wide range of goods and services at the drop of a hat, or amuse themselves any time, anywhere. To meet this demand, shops and places of entertainment have to be open late at night and on Sundays. Technology encourages this trend: the virtual economy of the internet never sleeps.

The widening range of types of work also reflects long-term demographic trends, especially the greater number of women workers and longer life expectancy. Some see non-typical jobs as a necessary evil, while others, especially women with children, welcome the change.

The divide between traditional kinds of work and the new jobs is no longer watertight. People are increasingly switching back and forth between the two categories. In the course of a lifetime, a person may change from full-time to part-time work, from an office job to home office and from the security of a big firm to the adventure of entrepreneurship.

Changes in the nature of work are also breaking down the rigid frontiers which marked off the world of work. The traditionally distinct fields of work, education and leisure are now interwoven and coexist flexibly in a kind of triple helix of social life.

The emerging intangible and relational economy has a huge potential for growth because it is not bound by the constraints of material scarcity. However, the transition to the new economy is an open-ended process. The state has a key part to play in bringing it about. Governments can slow down the rate of change by making it more painful and more costly.

Obstacles to Change

Pessimistic scenarios are still plausible, such as that of an economy which generates few new jobs and is polarized between a small elite and the rest of the population who are marginalized and lie in precarious conditions. There is a big risk that this scenario will come to pass because current laws and regulations, as well as widespread pessimistic ideas about work, are powerful obstacles to change. Optimistic scenarios require a wholesale reform of institutional structures and profound changes in behaviour and attitudes. Such far-reaching changes often run into strong opposition from the social and political establishment and come up against the weight of psychological and social tradition. But the gamble of a new approach to work must be made if the transformation to the intangible economy is to succeed.

Chapter—41

From Revenge to Reparation

Penal policy takes a new direction by confronting offenders with the consequences of their acts and giving them a chance to make amends. Over the past few decades, more attention has been focused on the victims of crime than on criminals. This raises two questions. How far do legal systems take into account victims demands for justice in the sentences they mete out to offenders? And to what extent do sentences respond to those demands?

Eighteenth-century theories of law and justice developed by the englishtenment philosophers in Europe from the basis of what is now regarded as classical penal procedure, whose non-arbitrary character is quite different from the procedure that prevailed before the French Revolution. Many forms of corporal punishment disappeared and were replaced by simple, clear-cut punishments like fines and prison sentences.

In the nineteenth century, the purpose of prison sentences was to make criminals pay their debt to society. Incarceration temporarily kept offenders out of the way while serving as an example and a warning. Imprisonment was also supposed to give offenders time to reflect on their misdeeds.

With the citizens' safety uppermost in mind, classical penologists emphasized a strictly legal definition of crime and punishment. However, as a result of the growing influence of the behavioural sciences views of delinquency changed and the idea that a single sentence is appropriate for all offenders regardless of the crime committed came under attack. A new trend emerged whereby sentencing was required to take each offender's circumstances and personal history into account. Sentencing criteria were no longer based on the legal definition of the crime but on the threat to society posed by the offender. A battery of alternatives to fit specific individuals and situations were developed from the late nineteenth century onwards including prison terms for hardened criminals, suspended sentences and probation for occasional offenders and protective and rehabilitation systems for young delinquents. Sentences were seen as a useful means of reintegrating the criminal into society.

Crowded Prisons

After the Second World War and the 1948 Declaration of Human Rights, new alternatives to prison opened up prospects of more humane sentencing with a view to reintegrating offenders into society. But these hopes came to nothing and alternative sentences remained by and large marginal. Imprisonment did not become a solution of last resort.

In the 1970s, the flagrant inhumanity of correctional facilities, the psychological impact of incarceration and the social exclusion resulting from this form of Punishment resulted in a growing skepticism about the prison system's capacity to rehabilitate inmates. In many facilities they also led to strikes, revolts and uprisings, which were sometimes violently put down.

Since the 1980s, two opposing viewpoints have emerged. On the one hand, prison seems to have lost its legitimacy as a punitive institution. On the other, some organisations insist that inmates serve out their full sentences, thereby restoring the punitive function of imprisonment. At the same time, those who remain unconvinced of the socializing virtues of deprivation of deprivation of freedom stress that, in a democratic state under the rule of law, inmates are citizens entitled to legal protection and basic human rights.

Over the past ten years, crowded prison conditions have overshadowed ideological discussions about the appropriateness, usefulness and humanness of incarceration. The average length of sentences has increased and procedure for early release have become more complicated. Keeping the offender off the streets seems to have become the main purpose of imprisonment.

The Debate on Sentencing

One major innovation that has emerged over the past two decades is the idea of reparation. Recent studies of the victims of crime have strongly influenced the debate on sentencing. The question of how far sentences solve the problems of victims is increasingly being asked. In this context the definition of criminality and the penal approach to it become part of a horizontal exchange relationship between offenders and victims Both are equally concerned in the solution that is found for the problem posed by a criminal offence.

Numerous offender-victim conciliation projects show that this is in many cases a realistic approach and, what is more, highly satisfactory for both parties and effective in changing the offender's behaviour. Conciliation plays a major role in helping to build a criminal justice system in which offenders make some amends to their victims.

In handing out prison terms, little attention was given to the victim. An intelligent execution of the sentence should take into consideration how the offender and victim experienced the crime. The systematic denial of the meaning and consequences of the offence and its acceptance or rejection by victims and offenders strongly dehumanizes the application of the sentence. Confronting offenders with the consequences of their deeds and giving them an opportunity to make amends should become a basic function and priority of the criminal justice system in the very near future. In a society where attention is now focused on the victim, sentencing which does not require offenders to make amends to their victims lacks credibility and meaning.

Chapter—42

The Electronic Gap

In the United States, business journals, market gurus, economics professors and highly paid consultants talk incessantly about the coming global boom, the transformation of the workplace, the technology revolution and the knowledge explosion. It is implied that the world is slowly becoming a reproduction of Silicon Valley. It is asserted that this is the future. But instead of swallowing this hype, perhaps we should pull back and look at the globe as a whole.

The pessimistic view would be to point out what is currently occurring in Kosovo, West Africa, Rwanda, Chechnya, Kashmir and elsewhere. We might also follow Robert Kaplan in the trips he describes in *To the Ends of Earth,* only to discover that much of humanity is headed for disaster and self-destruction. I do not wish to be as negative as that. However, I would like to offer a caution to those who portray globalization in an uncritical and overly enthusiastic manner.

One in three Americans are regular, daily internet users. Even within American society, the computer and e-mail have widened the gap between educated people (chiefly whites and Asians) and the less educated (chiefly black Americans). This gap will be felt in every aspect of life, whether it is in opportunities, potential, education or job-hunting The United States will be divided into two groups, one which is computer-literate and the other which is not.

This phenomenon has been replicated at the international level. The most important fact is that we are in the midst of a technology revolution that sees less likely to close the gap between rich and poor countries than to wide the gap even further.

The technology revolution and the communications revolution still bypass billions of human beings. The internet may have more influence than any single medium upon global educational and cultural developments in the coming century. Yet only 2.4 per cent of the world's population is on the internet, or one person out of 40. In Southeast Asia, only one person in 200 is linked to the internet. In the Arab states, only one person in 500 has internet access, while in Africa only one person in a 1,000 is an internet user This situation will not change as long as those lands lack electricity, telephone wires and infrastructure. They cannot afford either computers or the expensive software they require. If knowledge indeed equals power, the developing world may have less real power nowadays than it did 30 years ago, before the internet was developed.

If we want to work toward a knowledge-based society in the coming century, over at least the next 10 years we need to make a concerted effort to bring poorer societies into the system of electronic communications. This effort will need to be coordinated by the World Bank, the UN Development Programme, UNESCO, the NGO community and the global business community.

The alternative is to perpetuate a world is fundamentally undemocratic and structurally unsound. If we do nothing, if we let the knowledge explosion intensify in technology rich societies while poorer societies fall further behind, the growing gap between haves and have-nots will lead to widespread discontent and threaten any prospect of global harmony and international understanding. This is the most significant challenge we face. We have no time to waste in responding

Bibliography

Agarwal, Bina, 1992, "Gender Relations and Food Security: Coping with Seasonality, Drought and Famine in South Asia." In Lourdes Beneria and Shelley Feldman, eds. *Unequal Burden: Economic Crises, persistent Poverty, and Women's Work.* Boulder, Colo.: Westview Press.

Agarwal, Bina, 1997, "Bargaining and Gender Relations: Within and Beyond the Household." *Feminist Economics* 3(1): 1-51.

Akerlof, George A., and Rachel E. Kranton.,1999, *Economics and Identity.* Washington, D.C.: Brookings Institute.

Alkire, Sabina, 1999. "Operationalizing Amarty Sen's Capability Approach to Human Development: A Framework for Identifying 'Valuable' Capabilities." Ph. D. diss., Oxford University.

Baulch, Bob, 1996a, "Neglected Trade-Offs in Poverty Measurement." *IDS Bulletin* 27(1): 36-46.

Baulch, Bob, 1996b, "The New Poverty Agenda: A Disputed Consensus." *IDS Bulletin* 27(1): 1-10.

Bebbington A., and T. Perreaul, 1999, "Social Capital, Development and Access to Resources in Highland Ecuador." *Economic Geography.* October.

Beneria, Lourdes, 1989, "Gender and the Global Economy." In Arthur MacEwan and William Tabb, eds. *Instability and Change in the Global Economy.* New York: Monthly Review Press.

Berelson, Bernard, 1954, "Content Analysis." *Handbook of Social Psyc.. logy.* Vol. 1. Reading, Mass.: Addison-Wesley.

Bhatt, Mihir, 1999, "Natural Disasters as National Shocks to the Poor and Development." Disaster Mitigation Institute, Ahmedabad, India.

Booth, David, Jeremy Holland, Jesko Hentschel, Peter Lanjouw, and Alicia Herbert, 1998, *Participation and Combined Methods in African Poverty Assessment: Renewing the Agenda.* Department for International Development (DFID), U.K.: Social Development Division and Africa Division.

Bradley, Christine, 1994, "Why Male Violence against Women is a Development Issue: Reflections from Papua New Guinea." In Miranda

Davies, ed. *Women and Violence: Realities and Responses, Worldwide*. London: Zed Books.

Brunetti, Aymo, Gregory Kisunko, and Beatrice Weder, 1997, "Institutions in Transition: Reliability of Rules and Economic Performance in Former Socialist Countries." Policy Research Working Paper 1809, Washington, D.C.: World Bank.

Carvalho, Soniya, and Howard White, 1997, "Combining the Quantitative and Qualitative Approaches to Poverty Measurement and Analysis: The Practice and the Potential." Technical Paper 366. Washington, D.C.: World Bank.

Castellas, Manuel, 1997, *The Power of identity*. Malden, Mass.: Blankwell Publishers.

Cernea, Michael, 1979, "Entry Points for Sociological Knowledge in the Project Cycle." Agricultural and Rural Development Department. Washington, D.C.: World Bank.

———, ed., 1985, *Putting People First*. New York: Oxford University Press.

Cernea, Michael, with the assistance of April Adams, 1994, "Sociology Anthropology and Development: An Annotated Bibliography of World Bank Publication 1975-1993." Environmentally and Sustainable Development Studies and Monograph Series 3. Washington, D.C.: World Bank.

Cernea, Michael, and Ayse Kudat, 1997, "Social Assessments for Better Development: Case Studies in Russia and Central Asia." Environmentally Sustainable Development Studies and Monograph Series 16. Washington, D.C.: World Bank.

Chambers, Robert, 1989, "Editorial Introduction: Vulnerability, Coping and Policy." *IDS Bulletin* 20: 1.

Chambers, Robert, 1994, "The Origins and Practice of Participatory Rural Appraisal." *World Development* 22(7). Washington, D.C.: World Bank.

Chambers, Robert, 1997, "Whose Reality Counts?: Putting the First Last," London: Intermediate Technology Publications.

Chambliss, Villiam J., 1999, *Power, Politics, and Crime*. Bounder, Colo.: Westview Press.

Charmes, Jacques, 1998, "Informal Sector, Poverty and Gender: A Review of Empirical Evidence." Contributed paper for *World Development Report 2000*. Washington, D.C.: World Bank. October.

Dahle, Cheryl, 1999, "Social Justice-Alan Khazei and Vanessa Kirsch." Fast Company, Issue 30, December 1999, www.fastcompany.com.

Dasgupta, Partha, and Ismail Serageldin, 1999, *Social Capital: A Multifaceted Perspective*. Washington, D.C.: World Bank.

Davies, Miranda, ed., 1994, *Women and Violence: Realities and Responses Worldwide*, London: Zed Books.

Doller, David, and Roberta Gatti, 1995, "Gender Inequality, Income, and Growth: Are Good Times Good for Women?" Policy Research Report on Gender and Development, No.1 Washington, D.C.: World Bank.

Economist Intelligence Unit, 1997, *Armenia Country Profile, 1996-97*. London: The Economist Intelligence Unit, Ltd.

Edwards, Michael, and David Hulme, eds., 1992, *Making a Difference: NGOs and Development in a Changing World*. London: Earthscan Publications.

Edwards, Robert, and Michael W. Foley, 1997, "Social Capital and the Political Economy of Our Discontent." *American Behavioural Scientist*, 40(5): 669-78.

Esman, Milton, J., and Norman Uphoff, 1984, *Local Organizations: Intermediaries in Rural Development*. Ithaca, N.Y.: Cornell University Press.

Fajnzylber, Pablo, David Lederman, and Norman Loayza, 1998, *What Causes Violent Crime?* Office of the Chief Economist, Latin America and the Caribbean Region. Washington, D.C.: World Bank.

Floro, Maria Sagrario, 1995, "Economic Restructuring, Gender and the Allocation of Time." *World Development 23: 1913-29*. Washington, D.C.: World Bank.

Folbre, Nancy, 1991, "Women on Their Own: Global Patterns of Female Headship." In Rita S. Gallin, Anne Ferguson, and Janice Harper, eds. *The Women and International Development Annual*. Vol. 4. Boulder, Colo.: Westview Press.

Foley, Michael W., and Robert Edwards, 1996, "The Paradox of Civil Society." *Journal of Democracy* 7(3):38-52.

Foster, James, and Amartya Sen, 1997, "On Economic Inequality after a Quarter Century." 2nd ed. Oxford: Clarendon Press.

Fox, Jonathan, 1993, *The Politics of Food in Mexico: State Power and Social Mobilization*. Ithaca: Cornell University Press.

Galtung, Johan, 1994, *Human Rights in Another Key*. Cambridge, U.K.: Polity Press.

Gelles, Richard J., and Murray Straus, 1988, *"Intimate Violence."* New York: Simon and Schuster.

Giddens, Anthony, 1984, *"The Constitution of Society."* Oxford: Blackwell.

Goetz, Annne Marie, 1998, "Women in Politics and Gender Equity on Policy: South Africa and Uganda." *Review of African Political Economy* 76:241-62.

Greeley, Martin, 1994, "Measurement of Poverty and Poverty of Measurement." *IDS Bulletin 25(2)*.

Grootaert, Christiaan, 1998, "Social Capital: The Missing Link?" Social Capital Initiative Working Paper No. 3. Social Development Family. Washington, D.C.: World Bank.

———, 1999, "Social Capital, Household Welfare, and Poverty in Indonesia." Policy Research Working Paper 2148. Social Development Family. Washington, D.C.: World Bank.

Grootaert, Christiaan and Deepa Narayan, 1999, "Local Institutions, Poverty and Household Welfare in Bolivia." Social Development Family. Environmentally and Socially Sustainable Development Network. Washington, D.C.: World Bank.

Holland, Jeremy, and James Blackburn, eds., 1998, *Whose Voice? Participatory Research and Policy Change*. London: Intermediate Technology Publications.

Hyden, Goran, 1997, "Civil Society, Social Capital, and Development: Dissection of a Complex Discourse." *Studies in Comparative International Development* 32:3-30.

Jackson, Cecile, 1996, "Rescuing Gender from the Poverty Trap." *World Development* 23:489-504.

Jain, Devaki, 1996, "Panchayat Raj: Women Changing Governance." Gender in Development Programme. United Nations Development Programme, New York.

Kabeer, Naila, 1997, "Women, Wages and Intra-household Power Relations in Urban Bangladesh." *Development and Change* 28(2):261-302.

Kabeer, Naila, and Ramya Subrahmanian, 1996, *Institutions, Relations and Outcomes: Framework and Tools for Gender-aware Planning*, University of Sussex; U.K.: Institute of Development Studies.

Kaufmann, Georgia, 1997, "Watching the Developers: A Partial Ethnography." In R.D. Grillo and R.L. Stirrat, eds. *Discourses of Development: Anthropological Perspectives*. Oxford: Berg Press.

Korten, David C., 1990, *Getting to the 21st Century: Voluntary Action and the Global Agenda*. West Hartford, Conn.: Kumarian Press.

Krishna, Anirudh, and Norman Uphoff., 1999, "Mapping and Measuring Social Capital: A Conceptual and Empirical Study of Collective Action for Conserving and Developing Watersheds in Rajasthan, India." Social Capital Initiative Working Paper No. 13. Washington, D.C.: World Bank.

Krishna, Anirudh, Norman Uphoff, and Milton J. Esman (eds.), 1997, *Reasons for Hope: Instructive Experiences in Rural Development*. West Hartford, Conn.: Kumarian Press.

Leach, Melissa, Robin Mearns, and Ian Scoones, 1997, *Community-Based Sustainable Development: Consensus or Conflict?* University of Sussex, U.K.: Institute of Development Studies.

Lipton, Michael, and Martin Ravallion, 1995, "Poverty and Policy." In Jere Richard Behrman and Thirukodikaval Nilakanta Srinivasan, eds., *Handbook of Development Economics*, Vol. 3. Amsterdam: Elsevier Press.

MacEwen Scott, Alison, 1995, "Informal Sector or Female Sector? Gender Bias in Urban Labor Market Models." In Diane Elson, ed., *Male Bias in the Development Process.* 2nd ed. Manchester, U.K.: Manchester University Press.

Marshall, Gordon, 1994, *The Concise Oxford Dictionary of Sociology.* New York: Oxford University Press.

Max-Neef, Manfred, 1993, *Human Scale Development: Conception, Application, and Further Reflections.* London: Apex Press.

Milanovic, Branko, 1998, *Income, Inequality, and Poverty during the Transition from Planned to Market Economy.* Regional and Sectoral Studies, Washington, D.C.: World Bank.

Milimo, John T., 1995, "An Analysis of Qualitative Information on Agriculture: from Beneficiary Assessments, Participatory Poverty Assessments and Other Studies which used Qualitative Research Methods." Ministry of Agriculture, Food, and Fisheries. Lusaka, Zambia.

Moore, Mick, and James Putzel. "Thinking Strategically about Politics and Poverty." IDS Working Paper 101, University of Sussex, U.K.: Institute of Development Studies.

Moser, Caroline, 1998, *The Asset-Vulnerability Framework: Reassessing Urban Poverty Reduction Strategies.* Washington, D.C.: World Bank.

Moser, Caroline, Annika Tornqvist, and Bernice van Bronkhorst, 1998, "Mainstreaming Gender and Development in the World Bank: Progress and Recommendations." Washington, D.C.: World Bank.

Narayan, Deepa, 1999, "Bonds and Bridges: Social Capital and Poverty." Policy Research Working Paper 2167. Policy Research Department. Washington, D.C.: World Bank.

Narayan, Deepa, and Katrinka Ebbe, 1997, "Design of Social Funds: Participation, Demand Orientation, and Local Organizational Capacity." Discussion Paper No. 375, Washington, D.C.: World Bank.

Narayan, Deepa, and Lant Pritchett, 1999, "Cents and Sociability: Household Income and Social Capital in Rural Tanzania." *Economic Development and Cultural Change* (47)4:871-8.

Narayan, Deepa, and Lyra Srinivasan, 1994, *Participatory Development Tool Kit: Training Materials for Agencies and Communities.* Washington, D.C.: World Bank.

Narayan, Deepa, and Michael Cassidy, 1999, "A Dimensional Approach to Measuring Social Capital: Development and Validation of a Social Capital Inventory." Draft. Washington, D.C.: World Bank.

Narayan, Deepa, and Talat Shah, 2000, *Gender Inequity, Poverty, and Social Capital.* Policy Research Report on Gender Development, Working Paper Series. Washington, D.C.: World Bank.

North, Douglas, 1990, "Institutions and their Consequences for Economic Performance." In Karen Schweers Cook and Margaret Levi, eds. *The Limits of Rationality*. Chicago, Ill.: University of Chicago.

Norton Andy, and Thomas Stephens, 1995, "Participation in Poverty Assessments." Social Development Papers 9. Washington, D.C.: World Bank.

Orbach, Susie, 1999, "Psychoanalysis and Social Policy." Seminar paper presented to the World Bank, Washington, D.C.: April.

Patton, Michael Quinn, 1990, *Qualitative Evaluation and Research Methdos*, Newbury Park, Calif: Sage Publications.

Portes, Alejandro, 1998, "Social Capital: Its Origins and Applications in Modern Sociology." *Annual Review of Sociology* 22: 1-24.

Pottier, Johan, 1997, "Towards an Ethnography of Participatory Appraisal and Research." In R.D. Grillo and R.L. Strirrat, eds. *Discourses of Development: Anthropological Perspectives*. Oxford, U.K.: Berg Press.

Putnam, Robert, Robert Leonardi, and Raffaella Y. Nanetti, 1993, *Making Democracy Work: Civic Traditions in Modern Italy*. Princeton, N.J.: Princeton University Press.

Ravallion, Martin, 1995, "China's Lagging Poor Areas." *Amercian Economic Review, Papers and Procedures* 89:301-5.

Ray, Raka, and Anna Kortweg, 1999, "Women's Movements in the Third World: Identity, Mobilization and Autonomy." *Annual Review of Sociology* 25:47-71.

Rietbergen-McCracken, Jennifer, and Deepa Narayan, 1998, "Participatory Tools and Techniques: A Resoruce Kit for Participation and Social Assessment." Social Policy and Resettlement Division, Environment Department, Washington, D.C.: World Bank.

Robb, Caroline, 1999, "Can the Poor Influence Poverty? Participatory Poverty Assessments in the Developing World." Washigngton, D.C.: World bank.

Rodrik, Dani, 1998, "Globalization, Social Conflict and Economic Growth." *World Economy* 21(1):43-58.

Rupesinghe, Kumar, and Marcial Rubio, 1994, *The Culture of Violence*. New York: United Nations University Press.

Salmen, Lawrence, 1987, *Lisen to the People*. New York: Oxford University Press.

Salmen, Lawrence, 1995, "Participatory Poverty Assessment: Incorproating Poor People's Perspectives into Poverty Assessment Work." Social Development Paper No. 11, Washington, D.C.: World Bank.

Salmen, Lawrence, 1998, "Toward a Listening Bank: A Review of Best Practices and the Efficacy of Beneficiary Assessment." Social Development Paper No. 23, Washington, D.C.: World Bank.

Sartori, Giovanni, 1997. "Understanding Pluralism." *Journal of Democracy* 8(4):58-69.

Schuler, Sidney Ruth, Syed M. Hashemi, and Shamsul Huda Badal, 1998, "Men's Violence against Women in Rural Bangladesh: Undermined or Exacerbated by Microcredit Programmes?" *Development in Practice* 8(2):148-57.

Schwartz, S.H. 1994. "Are There Universal Aspects in the Structure and Contents of Human Values?" *Journal of Social Issues* 50(4):19-45.

Sen, Amartya K., 1981, *Poverty and Famines,* Oxford: Clarendon Press.

Sen, Amartya K., 1983, "Poor, Relatively Speaking." *Oxford Economic Papers* 35:153-69. Reprinted in *Resoruces, Values and Development.*

Sen Amartya K., 1984. "Rights and Capabilities." In Amartya K. Sen, ed., *Resources, Values and Development.* Oxford, U.K.: Blackwell.

Sen Amartya K., 1985, "A Sociological Approach to the Measurement of Poverty: A Reply to Professor Peter Townsend." *Oxford Economic Papers* 37:669-76.

Sen Amartya K., 1992, *Inequality Reexamined,* Cambridge, Mass: Harvard University Press.

Sen Amartya K., 1993. "Economic Regress: Concepts and Features." *Proceedings of the World Bank Annual Conference on Development Economics,* 315-54.

Sen Amartya K., 1997, *On Economic Inequality.* 2nd ed. Oxford: Clarendon Press.

Sen Amartya K., 1999. *Development as Freedom.* New York: Knopf Press.

Shah, Shekhar, 1999, "Coping with Natural Disasters: The 1998 Floods in Bangladesh." Seminar paper presented in June to the World Bank, Washington, D.C.

Shapiro, Gillbert, and John Markoff, 1997, "A Matter of Definition." In Carl W. Roberts, ed., *Text Analysis for the Social Sciences.* Mahwah, N.J. Lawrence Erlbaum Associates.

Silverman, David, 1993, *Interpreting Qualitative Data: Methods for Analyzing Talk, Text and Interaction.* Thousand Oaks, Calif.: Sage Publications.

Srinivas, Smita, 1999, *Social Protection for Women Workers in the Informal Economy.* Draft. Washington, D.C.: World Bank and Geneva: International Labour Office.

Standing, Guy, 1999, "Global Feminization through Flexible Labor: A Theme Revisited." *World Development* 3(27): 583-602.

Stone, P.J., D.C. Dunphy, M.S. Smith, and D.M. Ogilvie, 1966, *The General Inquirer: A Computer Approach to Content Analysis.* Cambridge: MIT Press.

Statuss, Anselm L., 1987, *Qualitative Analysis for Social Scientists*, New York: Cambridge University Press.

Tarrow, Sidney, 1994, *Power in Movement: Social Movements, Collective Action and Politics*. Cambridge, U.K.: Cambridge University Press.

Tendler, Judith, 1997, *Good Government in the Tropics*. Baltimore, Md.: John Hopkins University Press.

Townsend, Peter, 1971, *The Concept of Poverty*. London: Heinemann Educational.

Tripp, Aili Mari, 1992, "The Impact of Crisis and Economic Reform on Women in Urban Tanzania." In Lourdes Bereria and Shelly Feldman, eds., *Unequal Burden: Economic Crises, Persistent Poverty, and Women's Work*. Boulder, Colo.: Westview Press.

Uphoff, Norman, 1986, *Local Institutional Development: An Analytical Sourcebook with Cases*. West Hartford, Conn.: Kumarian Press.

Uphoff, Norman, Milton J. Esman, and Anirudh Krishna, 1997, *Reasons for Success: Learning from Instructive Experiences in Rural Development*. West Hartford, Conn.: Kumarian Press.

Visaria, Leela, 1999, "Violence against Women in India: Evidence from Rural Gujarat." In *Domestic Violence in India: A Summary Report of Three Studies*. Washington, D.C.: International Centre for Research on Women.

Weber, Robert Philip, 1990, *Basic Content Analysis*, 2d ed. Newbury Park, Calif.: Sage Publications.

WHO (World Health Organization)., 1997, *Violence against Women*, Geneva.

Woolcock, Michael, 1998, "Social Capital and Economic Development: Toward a Theoretical Synthesis and Policy Framework." *Theory and Society* 27(2): 151-208.

Woolcock, Michael, and Deepa Narayan, 2000, "Social Capital: Implications for Development Theory, Research, and Policy." *World Bank Research Observer* 15(2), Washington, D.C.: World Bank.

World Bank, 1996a. *From Plant to Market: World Development Report 1996*. Washington, D.C.

———, World Bank, 1996b, *Sourcebook on Participation*. Washington, D.C.

———, 1997a, *Poverty Assessment: A Process Review*. Operations Evaluation Department Document 15881. Washington, D.C.

———, World Bank, 1997a. *Poverty Assessment: A Process Review*. Operations Evaluation Department Document 15881. Washington, D.C.

———, World Bank, 1997b. *World Development Report 1997: The State in a Changing World*. New York: Oxford University Press (for the World Bank).

———, World Bank, 1998, *World Development Indicators,* Washigngton, D.C.

———, World Bank, 1999, *World Development Indicators,* Washington, D.C.

———, World Bank, 2000, *Poverty Trends and Voices of the Poor,* Poverty Reduction Group, Washington D.C.

Wratten, Ellen, 1995, "Conceptualizing Urban Poverty." *Environment and Urbanization* 7:11-36.

Index

G

H

I

L

R

V

W